The Green Heart
of the
Snowdrop

D1380376

The Green Heart

of the

Snowdrop

Kate McIlhagga

WILD GOOSE PUBLICATIONS

First published 2004 by
Wild Goose Publications
Fourth Floor, Savoy House, 140 Sauchiehall Street, Glasgow G2 3DH, UK

web: www.ionabooks.com

Wild Goose Publications is the publishing division of the Iona Community.
Scottish Charity No. SCO03794. Limited Company Reg. No. SCO96243.

ISBN 1 901557 85 5

A catalogue record for this book is available from the British Library.

Overseas distribution
Australia: Willow Connection Pty Ltd, Unit 4A, 3-9 Kenneth Road, Manly Vale, NSW
2093
New Zealand: Pleroma, Higginson Street, Otane 4170, Central Hawkes Bay
Canada: Bayard Distribution, 49 Front Street E. #200, Toronto, Ontario M5E 1B3

Printed by Cromwell Press, Trowbridge, Wiltshire, UK.

Contents

Open the stable door 75

Not for the faint-hearted 97

Dawn's ribbon of glory 123

Together on pilgrimage   147

The gentling of friends   165

In the ebb and flow   190

Introduction

I am writing this as the first snowdrops push their heads through the Northumberland snow. Soon they will reveal the green heart on the underside of their petals which so captured Kate's imagination. Like so much in nature, it symbolised for her some aspect of God's purpose for our lives, and finds an echo in this collection.

Kate was a wordsmith whose imagery and economy of language spoke to many people. Her ability to say a great deal in a few words gives the items in this book a distinctive style which takes our thought and imagination beyond ourselves to what she called 'an eternal source'. Some pieces are clearly prayers. Some are poems. Some, maybe all, are both. Most of the titles of the individual items are Kate's. I have grouped them into nine sections to which I have given theme titles drawn from the prayer-poems themselves. The sections inevitably overflow into each other and sometimes the decision about where to put a particular piece was not easy.

Much of the inspiration of *From the corners of the world* comes from Kate's gift of gathering people into friendship, something that has been nourished for us both over the last forty years in the life of the Iona Community. Kate was a welcoming person whose smiling eyes are recalled whenever people talk about her. This quality reflected her ability to lead people to an awareness of their potential healing and wholeness. She was in constant demand as a retreat leader and as a spiritual director, and appropriately for a number of years co-convened the Iona Community's working group on spirituality. This all contributes to the second section, *My soul waits*. I can remember her returning from an Ignation retreat where she had been intrigued by the idea of 'nourishing our own inner monasteries', while her regular participation in the Julian movement with its experience of shared silence taught her a lot about 'waiting'. Some of her thinking here reflects, of course, her own trials of a twenty-year battle with breast cancer over the whole period of her ordained ministry.

Much of *My soul waits* and most of *The greening of trees* owe much to Kate's passion for the integrity of creation. Most of her writing was done in the last ten years of her life and inspired by living in the 'secret kingdom' of Northumberland. She loved the Cheviot Hills as she loved walking on St Cuthbert's sands overlooking Holy Island, and she would visit Lindisfarne as often as she could. The clarity of light and its source in the heavens, the tides and their effects on the shoreline, the trees in their different seasons spoke to her of God's gracious action in surprising ways. In her earlier years, city life in Glasgow, in Edinburgh and Aberdeen, in Leeds and Sheffield, had perhaps a sharper cutting edge. That experience also finds reflection in the theme of creation's integrity.

Not just the turning seasons, but the parallel cycle of the Church's year spoke to her of the centrality of faith and hope and love. *Open the stable door* takes us from Advent through Christmas and New Year to Epiphany. *Not for the faint-hearted* continues our journey through the demanding time of Lenten wilderness, though including its halfway point when we celebrate and meditate on Mothering. Kate was a feminist in the best sense. A Mothering God and a Compassionate Spirit took her expression of the faith beyond issues of gender. In her own family life she was a very proud mother and grandmother, and I trust she rejoices that I have dedicated this book to our three sons, their wives and four grandsons. *Dawn's ribbon of glory* celebrates a resurrection life now. As a Christian Aid adviser Kate prayed and worked for 'life before death' for the least privileged of our world.

This 'justice and peace' theme, with its practical outworking in fair trade, flows into the next two sections. *Together on pilgrimage* owes much to our Celtic heritage, which, when she discovered Carmichael's *Carmina Gaedelica,* became one of the strongest influences on Kate's life and work – as she would often put it, 'prayer and politics are indivisible'. She was very conscious of the Company of Saints through the centuries, surrounding us as we pilgrimage in their steps – men and women, ancient and modern: Columba and Anna of Iona, Cuthbert and Hilda of Northumbria; but no less Elizabeth Fry and Luther King, Josephine Butler and Romero from nearer our day. *The gentling of friends* helps us to pray for others, often with a recurring theme of Kate's writing, 'hope'. Her embrace is as world-wide as it is inclusive of 'all conditions of humanity'. She was an ecumenist in the true sense of that word.

The final section, *In the ebb and flow*, is first an affirmation of 'every blessed thing'. One of her favourite sayings, which would often come through in her preaching – or as one friend put it when she retired, through 'the good stories that she told' – was that 'darkness and light are both alike to God'. Blessings are there in both. Endings too were a constant concern of hers, not least because she trained people who were involved in bereavement care. She started what is still a continuing care movement during our ministry in Huntingdonshire and latterly carried on this work with the day hospice in North Northumberland. Two of the last prayer-poems ('Death' and 'Surrounded by a Cloud of Witnesses') were used at her own 'Funeral Celebration' in April 2002 in the parish church of Norham, the village to which we had retired.

Kate had her favourite authors, and there are sometimes allusions in her prayer-poems to Eliot, to Hopkins, to Berrigan or Bonhoeffer, and she died with Eliot's echo of Mother Julian on her lips, 'All shall be well'. Her quotation from Bonhoeffer, 'Death is the last great festival on the road to freedom', demands that the final piece in this collection should be one about our destination, the one Kate entitled 'Trinity', ending as it does,

> 'The circle is complete ...
> God ever-living
> God ever-loving
> God ever-present
> in perfect community.'

Donald McIlhagga,
Candlemas 2004.

Kate's prayer-poetry was first published by the United Reformed Church in its Prayer Handbook for 1993, Encompassing Presence. *Since then her work has appeared in some thirty anthologies and in a number of liturgies published for special occasions. Requests for the use of the items in this book should be addressed to Wild Goose Publications.*

*This book is dedicated to
Malcolm, Kate, Sam and Jay;
Alasdair and Fiona; and Niall,
Stephanie, James and Peter.*

Poem – Prayer Prayer – Poem

Words bubbling up from an eternal source

phrases that haunt the corridors of the mind

until they are spilt, black on white

to form a pattern

a pleasing echo

gift of God

gifted back

to the Creator

From the corners of the world

Let us knock at God's gate with our prayers
(St Cuthbert)

As surely as seasons unfold
and Spring follows Winter
so surely is your steadfast love
O God.

As burns
released from Winter's bondage
leap joyously to the sea,
melt our frozen hearts
that we may worship you.

O come let us worship and bow down,
let us kneel before the Lord our maker,
for God it is who made us,
not we ourselves.

Womb dark and lifeless,
you knitted us with love.
Growing and grappling,
you grasped us with love.
Wandering and doubtful,
you held us with love.
Suffering and sickened,
you healed us with love.
Searching uncertainly,
you found us with love.
And in the following,
you lead us with love,
today, tomorrow and always.

At Alnmouth Friary

Dawn islands
emerge
from a silver sea;
an old stone floor,
jewel patterned,
a distant dove
and a bell
call to worship.

The sun places
a door-stop
of light
on the horizon
and bread
is broken
for the world.

New life*

Mysterious stranger,
unfolded from the womb
you drop into my arms
you open your eyes
meet mine
and recognition
sparks between us.
Love enfolds us both.

Well known one,
between one breath
and the next
unfolded from life
you slip away
through death's door
to be enfolded by love.

Written after a birth and a death.

Time

God of the past who has fathered and mothered us
we are here to worship you.
God of the future who is always ahead of us
we are here to trust you.
God of the present, here in the midst of us
we are here to praise you.

Let us worship God,
the God who forms the rhythm
of our lives,
the God who is present
at the beginning and ending
of each day … each time …
each purpose.

God of the longest day
may our lives be a long day for you,
always reflecting your light,
open and awake.

God of all time,
God beyond and behind time,
may we know what is too late
and what is too soon.
May we always recognise the right time
in the light
of your timeless love.

Welcome

When we are happy,
when we are full of fun and laughter
God welcomes us.
When we are angry,
when people let us down and make us sad
God welcomes us.
When we are tired,
when we need to stop and
curl up and rest
God welcomes us.

God of welcome,
God whose door is always open
we are glad to meet you here.

Gather us, O God,
that we may come
expectant to worship,
bringing with us
the pain and joy
of time that is past.

Grant that what we do
in your name
may be done
to your glory,
that justice and peace
may embrace,
love and faith unite.

Gathering

Let us keep silence
as we prepare to worship God
who is deep within us
and all around us

(Silence)

May our worship
touch the hearts and minds of all,
giving glory to God
through Christ
our brother.

From the corners of the world
from the loneliness of our hearts
from the confusion of our lives
gather us O God.

To feed our minds
to fire our imagination
to free our hearts
gather us O God.

A voice soft and musical
I pray for you;
a tongue loving and mild
I pray for you;
ears open and listening
I pray for you;
a mind clear and creative
I pray for you;

harmony and joy in singing
I pray for you.

Lord, in our praise
and in our prayer,
in our listening
and in our speaking,
may singer and song,
speaker and hearer,
become part
of the ongoing worship
of your eternal praise.

Living stones

Come as living stones,
the thumb-print of the mason
on each heart.

Come as living stones,
the imprint of the maker
on each soul.

Come as living stones,
the honing of life's suffering
on each mind.

Come to be made
into a house,
a community of God's purpose,
a place of habitation and welcome,
a place to come to
and a place to go from.

Teach us to number our days
(Ps. 90)

Bless to me, O God,
this day, fresh made.
Bless me in the lowing of cattle
and the rumble of traffic.
Bless me at desk or helm
and in the confines of my room.
Bless me in the comfort
       and constriction of my bed
and in the prayer I offer.

    Bless the unknown ones
    for whom I pray:
    the victims of terrorism
    and the perpetrators of it;
    those swept to extinction
        by fire or flood – thousands
        and yet each one known
        and precious to you.

Bless me in my journey, Christ
through this day
and through this life
till this day ends
and a new day dawns.

Open our lips

The Lord is a strong hold for the oppressed
a stronghold in times of struggle.
The needy shall not always be forgotten
nor the hope of the poor perish for ever.
Rise up O Lord.
Do not forget the oppressed.
O Lord open our lips
and we will declare our commitment.

Approach

Loving God,
out of our homelessness
we turn to you;
out of our helplessness
we come to you;
out of our hunger,
out of our pain
we return to you.

In love,
deep love
we come.
Stand beside us,
comfort our helplessness,
feed our hunger,
tend our pain,
hear our cry
and welcome us home.

Invocation

Come, let our hearts be glad
and our spirits rejoice,
for God has shown us the path of life
and leads us in the ways of peace.
May the seeds of hopefulness
be planted in our hearts today
and the fruits of hopefulness
blossom and grow within our community.

Come to us

God, Creator, Enfolder, Sustainer,
we come to you at the start of a new week.
    We come to you, bringing our joys and sorrows.
We come to you, knowing that your fingerprint is on each soul;
    that you have carved our names
    in the hollow of your hand.

God, Creator of the galaxies,
nearer to us than hands and feet,
we come to worship you.

(Silence)

Jesus says: those who come to me
I will not cast out …

(Silence)

Holy Spirit, Encourager,
come to us,
fill our worship
with your power and your love:
in the name of the Creator,
the Redeemer,
and the Sustainer.

Calling

O Christ, friend of sinners,
as you called men and women
into community with you,
call us to be your fisher people.
Gather us from our present occupation
to focus on the needs of your world.

Forgive us the pride and avarice
that keep us from you.
Forgive us the greed
that pollutes rivers and seas.
Forgive us the fear
that leads to war.

We give you thanks
for your love
which has brought us to faith;
your steadfast love
which has cradled a new creation;
your reconciling power
which has brought to birth
a new ministry.

God of light and warmth

O God, star kindler
kindle a flame of love within us
to light our path in days of darkness.

O God, sun warmer
warm us with your love
to melt the frozen hand of guilt.

O God, moonburnisher
burnish the shield of faith
that we may seek justice
and follow the ways of peace.

Invitation

The fire is lit,
the table set,
the door stands open.
Come to eat and drink,
come to be part of the community,
come to be part of a worldwide communion
of those who trust in Jesus.

Come round the table
saint and sinner,
stranger and friend,
to break bread
to share wine,
prepared and poured for you.

In sharing the symbols
of life blood spilt
and body broken,
become one with Christ
and with all those,
who, hurting,
yearn for healing today.

Come, here is food
for your healing,
bread and wine for your journey.
Come to be full-filled,
by God, the Giver and Lover of all.

My soul waits

Reflection

Make time to sit in comfort,
to breathe deeply,
to relax in the presence of God,
like a cat asleep on a chair
or a rabbit sunnily on a path:

> The Loving One, who made you,
> who yearned over you in the womb,
> who cherished you as a baby,
> who tended you as a child,
> who gave you glimpses of glory
>   from your pram;
> the One who moulded you,
> the One whose loving arm is always
>   under your head, says:
> *'Have no fear for I have*
>   *redeemed you.*
> *I call you by name*
>   *and you are mine.'*

I _____ AM LOVED BY GOD.

Keep silence in that thought.

Lord, teach us the silence of humility,
the silence of wisdom,
the silence of love,
silence that speaks without words,
the silence of faith.

Lord, teach us to silence our own hearts and minds, that we may listen
for the movement of your Holy Spirit, and feel your presence.

Give me a candle of the Spirit, O God,
as I go down into the depths of my being.
Show me the hidden things,
the creatures of my dreams,
the storehouse of forgotten memories.
Take me down to the spring of my life
and tell me my nature and my name.
Give me freedom to grow,
so that I may become that self,
the seed of which you planted in me
at my making.
Out of the deeps I cry to you, O God.

'Nourishing our own inner monasteries'

Let silence be placed around us
like a mantle.
Let us enter into it,
as through a small secret door;
stooping,
to emerge into
an acre of peace,
where stillness reigns
and God is ever present.

(Silence)

Then comes the voice of God,
in the startled cry
of a refugee child,
waking
in unfamiliar surroundings.

Then comes the voice of God,
in the mother,
fleeing with
her treasure
in her arms, and saying
'I am here.'

Then comes the voice of God,
in the father
who points to the stars
and says:
'There is our signpost.
There is our lantern.
Be of good courage.'

(Silence)

O Lord, may the mantle of silence
become a cloak of understanding
to warm our hearts in prayer.

Open

I stand.
I open myself to God.
I kneel.
I listen.
I step into God's presence.
I float in the encompassing ocean of God's love.
I breathe in and out:
breathing in the mercy of God,
breathing out the pain of my sadness.

I am still,
at rest with God,
who is deep within me
and all around me.

Out of that deep centre
I weave a prayer
of God's presence,
affirming that God is:
that God is with the poor,
that God is with the outcast,
that God is with me.

I call upon God's Spirit.
She rests like a butterfly
shimmering on a branch.
She confronts the hurt,
which lies twisted
at the heart of society.

> She leads me out
> from active prayer
> into prayerful action.

Creating, Sustaining and All-loving God,
give us the strength and courage to be still,
that we might better serve your broken world.

I am Mary and I am Martha

Read Luke 10:38–42 and then let God's Spirit pray through you:

Lord of earth and sky
as Martha did
I welcome you into the house of my heart;
as Mary did
I welcome you into the home of my thoughts.

> In service,
> in listening
> I welcome you.

Like Martha, I'm distracted:
so many calls on my time …
I run here and there
starting this and that,
never spending long enough,
giving people the impression
that I'm too busy for them.

Like Mary, I choose:
choose to slow down,
choose to sit at your feet,
choose to offer you
my ministry of listening.

Save me from feeling guilty
about the kitchens of the world:
the hot spots, the action areas
and help me to identify with your compassion
and your presence,
there as everywhere.

Welcomed and welcoming Christ
may all sisters come together
into your presence
and together eat at your table
the meal you have prepared for us,
that from the kitchen of your suffering
a banquet may be prepared
for all to eat.

The Word awaited

Sometimes
I long to call
words of praise
to me,
so that they may settle
like doves on my palm.
I long to coax them
down from the trees
into my waiting hands.

Sometimes they come,
swift and powerful
like hawks to the fist of the falconer,
words of challenge,
fierce words of regret.

One time you came,
The Word;
not at my call.
You came
to occupy
a cradle,
a grave,
my heart,
a universe.

You came to call me
to unleash
words of comfort,
words of hope.

Sometimes
I hold out
my empty hands
and wait.

My soul waits

I wait …
for pain to subside,
for fear to recede …
I wait …
for a home …
a job …
a friend …
for results to come,
a letter,
a call;
for the tide to turn.
I wait for hope
to return,
for joy
to slide again
into my life.
I wait
for the Lord.

Marie Curie

The tireless dark
presses against the pane,
as feet sluggish
heavy minded
drag
through the weary days
until
one bird sings,
one green-hearted snowdrop
cries – palely defiant
and I
turn
to embrace
the pain.

Dark and bright

Out of my dark days
float
long lost sambas
and forgotten dreams.

Hopes dashed ...
fears realised ...
pain abounding ...

Out of my bright days
float
memories of picnics
and melons eaten knee deep
in a hidden loch.

Hopes realised ...
fears confronted ...
joy enflooded ...

Dark and bright
day and night
all are held
in the hands
of a loving God.

Help me to see the connections
welcome the intertwinings
let go the pain and embrace the future.

The fir tree

At the tip
of the tallest fir tree
there is a shoot,
a fragile shoot
waving in the wind.

From desolation to consolation;
from consolation to desolation;

but
underneath
for many feet
is a strong, long,
sturdy trunk,
deeply rooted
supporting
holding;
affirming
I am part of the tree.

Shepherd King

Shepherd King,
as you looked lovingly
into the eyes
of the rich young man,
look on me.

God's anointed,
as you looked searchingly
into the heart
of King David,
look on me.

As I drift heedless
into the false calm
of a life lived
within the confines
of others' expectations,
save me from shipwreck.

As I tremble
before the next task,
strengthen me.

Help me to take on the giants in my life;
to battle with conscience
and the dictates of culture.

Then may I
look into your eyes
and offer you
all that is most precious,
as I receive your gift
of life in all its fullness.

Prepare the way

Universal giver of bread and breath,
where our hearts are cold,
where our spirits are lifeless,
you call us to repentance.
Breathe your life-giving spirit into us,
feed us with the bread of life
and renew us for your service.

Christ, saviour of humankind,
where the life of the world is burdened by our sin,
where your people are broken-hearted,
you call us to repentance.
Help us to prepare the way for you,
build highways for you
and clear the rubble from our own doorstep.

Holy Spirit, giver of life,
where we grope after false ideals,
where we chase illusory goals,
you call us to repentance.
In shame, deep shame,
we turn to you
confessing our sin.

(Silence)

Forgiving God, forgive us.
Saving God, save us.
Living God, give us new life.

Confession

Out of my pain
I confess my hate-filled days.
Out of my anger
I confess my wish for revenge.

Out of my fear
I confess my distortion of the truth.

    O God who knows us in our weakness
    and befriends us in our chaos,
        free me from hate and fear;
    turn pain and anger
    into tools for healing;
    open the door to reconciliation
    and restitution of right relationships
    between friends and neighbours,
    between nations and peoples,
    that your truth may reign
    in our hearts,
    and your peace
    welcome us home.

Father forgive

'Father forgive, they do not know what they are doing.'

For all the times we have acted without love,
    Father forgive.
For all the times we have acted without thought,
    Father forgive.
For all the times we have withdrawn support,
    Father forgive.
For all the times we have failed to forgive,
    Father forgive.

For the hurt of the world, of which we are a part,
for the brokenness of society to which we contribute,
for the disunity of the Church, to which we belong,
    may God forgive us,
    Christ renew us,
    and the Spirit enable us
    to grow in love.

Too easy

How can we seek the warm safety of worship,
when so many are alone and afraid?

O loving God,
help us to find worship
a sending and strengthening,
not to seek it
as an analgesic or an avoidance.

For expecting too much,
for expecting too little,
GOOD LORD, FORGIVE US.

> For making easy promises
> and failing to keep them,
> *GOOD LORD, FORGIVE US.*

For hasty words and thoughtless actions,
for easy answers and careless thinking,
GOOD LORD, FORGIVE US.

> For avoiding the hurt of the world
> and ignoring the needs of others,
> *GOOD LORD, FORGIVE US.*

Those who seek shall find.
Those who ask for forgiveness
are forgiven.

Promises

For the promises I have made
then broken,
forgive me, Lord.
Of my outward show
and inward poverty,
heal me, Lord.
In my desire to produce fruit
and in my struggle,
help me, Lord.

The grey cloud

There have been times
when having the energy
to strike a match
to light a candle
and to pray
that tomorrow is another day
has not been possible.

In those day times
those grey times
help me to do the next thing
lovingly,
the next thing
carefully,
the next thing
joyfully.

Then break through the cloud
of my despair
that I may see
the things of beauty
by which I am
surrounded.

Desperate companion

Despair is a desperate companion
for facing the unknown.

Much rather the funny, dancing
loving partner of my journey,
the spirit of sparkling hope
to lighten my load
and wash away my tears.

Perhaps I'm searching in
the wrong place,
asking the wrong questions.

O God, midwife of my life,
deliver me from anxiety,
dispel my fear,
calm my racing heart,
bring hope to birth again.

Heart search

Patient Lord,
you bear with me in my slowness to understand;
forgive my excuses,
transform my mistakes,
and lead me in your way.

> *Lord Jesus Christ*
> *Son of the living God,*
> *have mercy on me,*
> *a sinner.*

Humble Christ,
you go down with me into the waters of baptism;
forgive my hesitation,

cleanse my sinfulness,
and bring me new life in you.

> *Lord Jesus Christ*
> *Son of the living God,*
> *have mercy on me,*
> *a sinner.*

Gracious Spirit,
you become one with me as I seek freedom;
forgive my disobedience,
transform my allegiance.

> *Lord Jesus Christ*
> *Son of the living God,*
> *have mercy on me,*
> *a sinner.*

The Holy One of Israel,
the Shepherd King, born in Bethlehem,
the Dove hovering over the waters of our chaos,
forgive us and set us free
from all that harms us.

Help us to admit our emptiness
(Based on the story of the Prodigal)

Spirit hovering over our chaos,
help us to acknowledge our sin;
lead us to deeper repentance in unity with Christ.
Help us to admit our emptiness
that we may turn to be filled
with the love that rushes to meet us.

May we be more conscious of God's goodness
than of our own guilt.
May we allow ourselves to be embraced and kissed
by the father, who delights in us,
and if we look out of the eyes of the other,
the elder brother, in jealousy and pain,
help us to admit our emptiness
that we may turn to be filled
with the love that says:
'My son, my daughter,
you are with me always,
and all I have is yours.'

When we see the happiness of father and children
through the smoke of the cooking fire,
from behind the daily juggling act of unfinished tasks,
may our tears be ones of joy,
as we admit our emptiness,
our longing for fulfilment,
and receive the understanding love
which empowers and enables us
to serve by being ourselves.

Shepherd and sheep

As a shepherd
seeks the lost sheep;
as a woman searches for the lost coin;
Parent God, seek and search for us,
for we have wandered far from home.
We have lost touch
with what nourishes and stretches us.
We have missed the mark,
aiming at false security
instead of seeking the goal of the Kingdom.
We have preferred prosperity
to the cutting edge of life lived in your presence.
We have bowed down to the idol of expediency
and neglected to tend the gifts of the Spirit.

Christ, who makes whole,
bring us back from the precipice.
Holy Spirit, who leads us into all truth,
bring us home to God.

Sheep among wolves

Enticing Presence,
as you burn within me,
save me from burnout.

Overpowering Love,
as you send us out,
save us from the wolfish lure of power,
the snarling wolves of selfishness.

Christ, Sender and Saviour,
as you travel with me,
save me from the wiles of complacency.

Christ our Teacher,
as you draw us on,
save us from the temptation of expediency,
the expedient use of resources.

Spirit of Humility,
as you work within me,
save me from the pride of humility.

Spirit of Discipleship,
as we are moulded by our trials,
save us from claiming our own strength
and grant us the gift of discerning speech.

Through the windows of our tears,
may we see you at work,
disturbing the peace,
embracing the pain of the universe
and calling us to costly service.

The flooding tide

Word of God, flowing free,
flow in and through us,
to cleanse and bring
a new beginning,
a fresh start,
right relationships
and peace.

> When the tide recedes,
> leaving a fresh page of sand,
> then the time is right for forgiveness.

When the tide is balanced on the horizon,
flowing in on one shore and out on another,
then the time is right for dialogue.

> When the tide comes flooding in,
> washing clean the beach,
> then the time is right to begin again.

(Silence)

Word of God, flowing free,
flow in and through us,
to cleanse and bring
a new beginning,
a fresh start,
right relationships
and peace.

Seeking harbour

As the grey wave
creeps on to the shore
and the sail limps
for port,
so, Lord, do I
seek harbour,
crawl into the circle
of your welcoming arms.

May I know your forgiveness.
Then may I forgive
as you have forgiven
me.

And now the blue comes flooding in,
transforming sea and sky with light;
the white wave tops
are bracelets of glory;
the sand
a new page
on which to write my story.

To know you in all things

Weave a web of your presence around me today.
Be with my hands as they work.
Be with my eyes as they see.
Be with my ears as they hear.
Be with my tongue as it speaks.
Be with my feelings and my thoughts.
Be with the people I meet.
Be with the things I make.
Be with the decisions I take.
Be in and through,
over and under all,
that doing and hearing and seeing,
speaking and making and being,
I may glimpse your glory,
hear your voice
and joyfully work with you
to create a new heaven and a new earth.

The greening of trees

Creator of all

Creator of the galaxies,
Ruler of the uttermost reaches of space,
You are nearer to us than hands and feet,
closer to us than our next breath.

We sense your Presence
in the tightly curled rosebud
and in the open arms of a golden beach.
We hear you in the sound of wind and waves
and in the soft chatter of happy children.
Your Presence is woven into the life of the world
and into our lives
and we are glad to sing your praise.

Rhythm of life

Darkness
curling round the edge of space
like mist on a summer morning
meets dancing light,
to touch and separate,
to embrace and part,
on that first day
of God's creating.

So in the rhythm
of our lives
must joy and sadness
weave a pattern
of God's purpose:
touch and tinge
our lives
with sorrow
and gladness.

Loved into being

Loved into being,
   hill, fen and field;
loved into being,
   ocean flood and fish;
loved into being,
   each plant and each tree;
loved into being,
   you and me.

Moonlight

Lovely new moon
holy be each thing
her eye lights on,
kindly be each deed
she reveals.

Moonlight,
lamplight of God,
compass us about
with the shield of your love.

Starlight

Bright shining star,
blessed be each thing
your eye lights on.
Radiant summer sun,
blessed be each thing
your smile touches.
As night and day
you warm and bless us,
so one day
shall the Lord, your creator
be our everlasting Light.

Son of God,
work in me
and through me
that I may shine
like the stars.
Shine through me
that I may reflect
your glorious light,
and sharing a sense of wonder
may point the way to God.

Spirit of God,
coax me from my hiding place.
Draw me out
to witness to God's love.
Restore my zest for life
that all that I do
may be to your glory.

Thanksgiving hymn

For lambs that leap
and birds that sing,
for every blessed glorious thing
that God has made
and loves and keeps,
we thanks and praises bring.

Each smile exchanged,
new thoughts, sweet dreams,
for every blessed glorious thing
that God has made
and loves and keeps,
we thanks and praises bring.

For Jesus Christ
our loving friend,
made, loved and kept
that we may sing
to praise our glorious king,
we thanks and worship bring.

(Based on Mother Julian)

Adoration

We cannot tell
how much the sound of silence,
creation's beauty, gloriously aflame,
moves us to prayer;
we cannot tell
how much the sight of starlit heavens
calls us to praise creation's maker,
and our own.

We cannot tell
how much the son of Mary,
the Son of God upon a tree,
moves us to prayer;
we cannot tell
how much the man of sorrows
calls us to praise the One
who gives our life a meaning and a goal.

We cannot tell
how much the Spirit's comfort,
how much the wind of freedom,
how much the cry of human pain
moves us to prayer.
We cannot tell,
for words cannot contain
the love beyond all loves,
the truth
that in the end
there is
only
God.

Sand and rock

O Creator of the earth,
save us from the insecurity of sand;
sinking, shifting, sliding.

O Saviour of the world,
help us to build on rock;
stable, safe, sure.

O Renewer of life,
bring us to the promised land;
changed, reformed, rebuilt.

Laudate

For the generous gifts of a bountiful Creator
Praise the Lord all people:

Laudate.

For the outpouring of sun and rain
for seedtime and harvest
Praise the Lord:

Laudate.

For milk that quenches our thirst
and strengthens our bones
Praise the Lord:

Laudate.

For fish that feed us
and help us grow
Praise the Lord:

Laudate.

For eggs that grace our table
and send us out with energy
Praise the Lord:

Laudate.

For wheat that symbolises our unity
one loaf for all to share
Praise the Lord:

Laudate.

But most of all
for the present that comes
gift-wrapped in a baby's shawl;
for Christ – for Love
crucified, dead and risen;
for Love that comes again
like wheat that springs up green,
Praise the Lord:

Laudate.

Creator of the stars of night
Creator of the welcome dawn
Come to rescue us who fall
Come to make us whole and well.

Imperfect

The earth is full of your glory, O God.
The skylark sings your praises.
The leaping lamb is your joy.
The dark hills reflect your constancy,
and the changing tides your faithfulness.
But beneath the feather, the claw;
beside the pool, pollution.
The delicate snowflake
pierces the newborn lamb like a knife.
We need to acknowledge, O Lord
that all is not perfect in this garden of your creating.

Confession

Eternal God,
for the beauty of creation
we praise you.
With the unnamed longings of our hearts
we come to you.

Where we have denied or ignored your love,
forgive us.
Where we have broken faith with you
and those we love,
forgive us.

Where your world is damaged
by our neglect,
forgive us.

Take our neglect, our brokenness, our denial
and weave them into a new pattern.
Set us free from old ways.
Strengthen us to make amends
and help us to live again as whole people,
through the love of Christ the healer.

Breaking sea

The waves hurl themselves
at the shore
like chariots racing;
so I hurl myself
at you, O God,
for comfort and for peace.

The glorious light of your presence
lines the horizon,
but still the breakers come
grey
cold
wet,
topped with a froth of white.

You could drown in that,
sucked under
by the relentless power
of the sea.

The waves heave and surge,
as I toss and turn,
one minute open to hope,
the next overwhelmed with loss.

As your power created
the power of the sea;
as your calm
rests on the distant horizon,
may I rest in your peace
and choose to hope.

Holy and hurt

The earth is full of the grandeur of God.
Praise God, thrush and falcon!
Praise him lark and robin!
Praise God, bees and sun-drunk cats!
Praise him orchids and mirk-filled bats!
Praise God all nations!
Let all the people praise God's splendour!

Beneath the feather, the claw,
around the rose, the thorn,
beside the pool, pollution,
above the blue mountain, the cloud:
nature too wounds and is wounded.
Holy is the soil we walk on,
holy the place we despoil.

God of grandeur and grace,
where we have laid waste your creation,
        FORGIVE US.
Where we have hurt and wounded each other,
        FORGIVE US.
Where your laws and commandments lie broken,
        FORGIVE US.

Forgive us and restore us to your kingdom,
that renouncing
what separates us from you,
we may respond
childlike
to your love,
meeting the demands of faith
on our knees,
not counting the cost
or the pain of discipleship,
as we praise your holy name.

Prayer for peace

O God,
we sense your presence
in the circle of a golden bay,
in the curve of a distant hill.

We see you in the faces
    that smile lovingly into ours.
We feel you in the salt tang of the sea
    and in the countless grains of sand,
for you are all around us,
    you are deep within us.

We exult in your presence
and praise your holy name.

But a shadow lies across the hill,
    a deep stain seeps into the golden sand,
faces are transfixed by a horrendous light,
    shadows burned on buildings,
    and the land laid waste for years to come.

Your people are helpless,
        homeless and heartsick;
 your children cry at empty breasts,
    and still the world pours more money
        into making arms than holding hands;
still our greed pollutes the earth,
    still the consequences of our sin
        reach out across the generations.

O Trinity of love,
forgive us, that we may forgive one another.
Heal us that we may be people of healing,
and renew us that we may be makers of peace.
Through Christ, the Prince of Peace,
we pray.

Open and generous

For the joy of a fresh sunrise,
for the hope each new day brings,
for a love that knows no bounds,
we praise you
bountiful God.

But even as words of praise
pass our lips,
we know that we have not always lived
as those who are loved, forgiven and set free.

We have allowed ourselves
to be imprisoned by tradition,
captivated by habit,
limited by fear.

Through the healing power
of love made flesh,
make us whole,
to live and love
with open hearts
and generous spirits.

Supplication

O God,
the delicate balance of your creation
is slowly being stripped of its riches:

your streams of living water
are choked with chemicals;
your life-giving trees
droop and die.

Open our eyes to see, and our ears to hear
the cry of your creation.
Teach us its wonders.
Teach us to cherish and protect your world.
Teach us how to live in partnership
with all things,
that we may learn how to live
as one body in Christ –

dependent on each other's gifts,
sharing in each other's hopes.

Reconciliation as God's gift

We face each other
across a raw divide,
the chasm of our anger
filled with the bones
of old hatreds.

The wounded earth
spews out our greed
in acrid smoke.
The gaping wound cries out in pain.

The upward surge of birds in flight;
wheeling and dancing
in the sun,
the sound of geese
strung across an empty sky,
the scent of blossom on the wind,
gifts of a generous Creator,
to lift, to call, to heal.

Mist cleared

It's difficult
to lift eyes
to hills covered in mist;
to draw strength
from seas
that batter the shore,
but it's you, Lord,
who brings help.

You calmed storms,
dispersed mists of doubt,
and said:
'Peace, be still.'

A strange new landscape:
an inscape
of light and shadow,
hope and fear;
an undulating
roller coaster
of a life;
a chapter of surprises,
not to be hurried over
but savoured.

Ploughed ground

The deep curve of pattern
on a ploughed field;
    the wide sweep of sand
    on a rain-washed bay;
the arching hump
of a distant hill;
    all give glory to a Creator God.

The depth of our ingratitude,
the width of our selfishness,
the height of our indifference,
add to the pain of a broken world.

    O holy one, Creator of field and hill,
    Saviour of the lost,
    to our brokenness
    bring the healing of your Spirit;

deepen our awareness of your presence,
widen our knowledge of your mercy,
heighten our sense of your forgiveness,
    and bring us back
    to fullness of life.

Ploughed pattern;
gulls screaming,
circling;
deep, rich soil
turned and open
to receive
the seed of
tomorrow.

Creator God,
sow the seeds of your love
deep in the soil of our hearts.
Bring us to fulfilment
in your kingdom.

St Swithin's Day

In a world of seed-time and harvest
God's promises are to be trusted.
In a world of betrayal and fear
God's promises are to be clung to.
In a world of despair and disillusion
God walks beside the poorest
and carries the weakest.
Into His world wine is poured
for the healing of the nations.

The turning tide

The tide is turning, turning
the great circle, swooping, flowing
relentless, powerfully flooding,
covering the pock marks of sin,
rubbing out the past.

The tide is turning, turning,
running in gentle ripples over the sand,
lapping at the rocks,
slip-slapping reminders
of the immense ocean of God's love.

The tide is turning, turning;
the waves are receding.
Re-seed, O Lord, the good,
cast the bad into the fire of the past.
Wash away our fears
like messages written on the sand.

The tide is turning, turning,
flowing in full,
drawing out,

leaving the beach
washed and empty,
a clean page
ready to start again.

Touch of love

As winter trees
stretch out bare arms
to a dark sky,
I stretch out
in the darkness
to find the touch of love.

As snowdrops
turn their gentle faces
to the sun,
I long to find
in that warmth
the promise of peace.

As the forest fire
breaks the shell of the seed,
so may my pain
break the shell of isolation
that protects me
from myself.

In the security of darkness,
the warmth of sunshine,
the promise of fire,
may I blossom anew
in the miracle
of your saving love
O God.

May time

The greening of trees
the gentling of friends
laughter's healing art
and love's costly power
beckon and lead me onwards.

O God, star-kindler
kindle a flame of love within me
to lighten my path
in days of darkness.

O God, sun-warmer
warm me with your love
to melt the frozen hand
of guilt.

O God, moon-burnisher
burnish my shield of faith
that I may seek justice
and follow in the ways
of peace.

Circuit

I make my circuit
in the fellowship of my God,
on the machair, in the meadow,
on the cold heathery hill,
on the corner in the open,
on the chill windy dock,

to the noise of drills blasting,
to the sound of children asking.

I make my circuit
in the fellowship of my God,
in the city street
or on spring-turfed hill,
in shop-floor room
or at office desk.

God has no favourite places.
There are no special things.
All are God's and all is sacred.
I tread each day
in light or dark
in the fellowship of my God.

Be the sacred Three of glory
interwoven with our lives
until the Man who walks it with us
leads us home
through death to life.

Open the stable door

Advent hope

Now is the season of hope unfolding,
the dark winter season, when hope waits to be born.
Let us come before God with receptive and willing spirits.
May our souls magnify God's name,
and our spirits rejoice in God our Saviour.

Pregnant with hope

Now is the time of watching and waiting
a time pregnant with hope
a time to watch and pray.

Christ our advent hope,
bare brown trees,
etched dark across a winter sky,
leaves fallen, rustling,
ground hard and cold,
remind us to prepare for your coming;
remind us to prepare for the time
when the soles of your feet will touch the ground,
when you will become one of us
to be at one with us.

May we watch for the signs,
listen for the messenger,
wait for the good news to slip into our world, our lives.
Christ our advent hope,
help us to clear the way for you;
to clear the clutter from our minds,
to sift the silt from our hearts,
to move the boulders that prevent us meeting you.

Help us to make straight the highways,
to unravel the deception that leads to war,
to release those in captivity.
May sorrow take flight,
and your people sing a song of peace
and hope be born again.

Clear the way

Gracious God,
as the days shorten
and the pale wintry sun
bathes the sky with light,
so may our anxiety abate
and the warmth of your love
cleanse and purify our lives.

Promised One,
as ice skims the pond
and bright frost
gilds the leaf with glory,
may the clarity of your call
awaken us to new hope
and new beginnings.

Holy Spirit of transformation,
help us to clear the way
for the coming Christ-child.
As the red sun sinks behind black branches,
slip into our lives
and surprise us by the welcome warmth
of your coming.

Itching ears

Creator God of star and sea,
coming to us in the bright light of hoar frost,
touching us with the keen wind of your presence,
    in the coldness of solitary places,
    in the coldness of grief,
    in the coldness of isolation,
may your Word warn and warm us.

Word of God, present with us now,
whose coming we prepare for,
forgive us as we try to imprison you
within our traditions.
Our itching ears listen
only to what suits us.
Forgive our failure to choose hope
or to plant seeds of hopefulness.
Warn and warm us with your coming.

Baptising Spirit, forgiving and healing,
may we stop and listen
for the sound of angel voices,
stop and search for a star
to lead us to the living Word,
that we might be warmed
by his love,
and fed at his table.

Different drummer

Creator of the milk white moon that washes the land,
Creator of the bright star that guides us to Christ,
Creator of the welcome sun that floods the earth,
lead us in light and dark.
As day enfolds night and night gives birth to day,
comfort us with your presence.

Spirit of life,
as we traverse the teeming city,
travelling overhead and underground;
as we journey from one deadline to the next,
lead us in light and dark.
As night enfolds day and day gives birth to night,
may we walk to the tune of a different drummer.

Christ, refugee and traveller,
as John cried out in the wilderness,
as John baptised for the forgiveness of sins,
as John proclaimed your coming,
may we, in the strength of our baptism,
be receptive to your Advent voice.

Grant us courage
to confront injustice,
to make the crooked straight.
Grant us the hope of your presence
in our hearts and in our hands and in our world.

Make us aware

Merciful God, forgive
    that we fall asleep
    when you call us to watch and pray.
We fail to see the signs of your coming.

Christ our Saviour, forgive
    that we are not watchful,
    we do not choose hope,
    or plant the seeds of hopefulness.
We fail to see the signs of your coming.

Forgiving Spirit, forgive
    that in the rush of the Christmas season
    we forget to stop and listen for the sound of angel voices,
    we forget to stop and look for a star
    to guide us to Christ.
We fail to see the signs of God's presence.

    God over all
    Christ within us
    Spirit around us
    hear our prayer
    and send your messenger
    of peace to us and to your sleeping world.

Christmas tide

The day before Christmas Eve
an empty stable
bare, unwelcoming,
sits in an empty church.

    Soon the faithful, the curious,
    the hopeful will gather.
    Soon the church will be filled
    with warmth and praise:

soft candlelight,
children's voices,
the song of the frosty stars.

And then the stable will be transformed,
filled with glory,
crowded with the Christmas cast
of donkeys and sheep,
shepherds and kings,
Mary, Joseph and the Baby,
the Holy One of Israel,
asleep on the hay.

Transform our empty spaces
O Christmas God.
Fill the empty mangers of the world
with food.
Empty the cardboard boxes,
refuge of the lonely and despairing.
Bring warmth and light and shelter
to all who watch and wait this night.

In bar and bare hillside,
in barrio and back room,
in crowded flat and empty home
may we feel your presence
at our shoulder and in our hearts.

And when the crib is packed away,
the figures carefully clothed
in protective covering,
unwrap the swaddling bands,
unfold the truth,
release the message:

an empty stable –
He's not here.
He has risen.

Birth song

Soon, soon,
the Saviour of the world will be born:
born into the arms of a strong woman,
born into the cupped hands of a carpenter.

Soon, soon,
the Saviour of the world will be born:
born lowly to raise the humble,
born vulnerable to feed the hungry,
born strong to scatter the proud,
born to raise the poor from the dust.

The night the star shines
the light of the world will be born.
The night the angels sing
the shepherd of the flock will be born:
the Trinity eternal,
the hungry breastling
without a home in the world.

God our Creator
is opening a door for us.
The mountains will rejoice
and the waves of the sea will sing for joy,
for there is no holy one like him.

Each day, each night,
O light of our lanterns,
we will praise and adore you.
Each day, each night,
we will prepare a home
in our heart for you.
Each day, each night,
may the world prepare a cradle
of welcome for you.

Soon, soon,
the Saviour of the world
will be born.

Come Christmas God

When it's cold and wet
and we long for the light
    come Christmas.

Come to bring warmth and joy
to innkeepers and travellers,
to shepherds and kings;
Come to bring hope and peace
to refugees and security forces;
Come to comfort the lonely
and wipe the tear from the cheek
of those who are sad.

Immanuel – God with us,
let your light shine
into the dark recesses
of our minds and our cities.
Let your warmth
bring forth harvests of joy.
Let your peace
enter the hearts
of those who struggle and plot
for power and advantage over others.

Come, Christmas God,
    Christ-child of Bethlehem,
    Spirit of wonder,
    be born in us and your world
    once more
        that joy may be shared
        peace proclaimed
        and love abound.

Moontime of the winter

In the moontime of the winter,
when the sun redly rises;
in the moontime of the winter,
when the trees starkly stretch,
then, O Christ, you come:
softly as a gently falling snowflake,
with the lusty energy of a newborn boy,
the blood and pain of your coming
staining the distant horizon.

In the frost of the starlight,
when the sun gives way to moon;
in the frost of the starlight,
when the earth is turned to stone,
then, O Christ, you come:
slowly as the rhythm of the seasons,
quickly as the rush of cradling waters,
worshipped by the wise,
adored by the humble,
the ecstatic joy of your coming
heralding songs of peace.

Into the world of refugee and soldier,
the soles of your feet have touched the ground.
Into the world of banker and beggar,
the soles of your feet have touched the ground.
Into the world of Jew and Arab,
the soles of your feet have touched the ground.

Walk with us, saviour of the poor,
be a light on our way,
travel beside the weary,
fill the broken-hearted with hope
and heal the nations,
that all may walk
in the light of the glory of God.

Northumbrian nativity

O Lowly Christ
on the darkest night of the year
the Christmas moon
has laid a pathway
across the sea for you
and the lighthouse
beams a welcome.

As sister moon gives way to brother sun
the Prince of Peace is crowned;
cries of pain give way to tears of joy
as Mary cradles the whole world in her arms.

A little child, a little child,
the living waters of Ezekiel
on Mary's knee.
O Saviour dear,
wise child of Isaiah,

help us to have
the humility of the shepherds,
the wisdom of the wise,
the steadfast love of Joseph
and the courage of Mary.

O Alpha and Omega on Mary's knee,
as your arm lifts the head of the guilty
help us to forgive.
As your hands caress the face of the poor
help us to seek justice.
As you kiss the leper clean
help us to know your peace.

O little child, shoot of Jesse,
promised one,
as we leave the stable,
as we go from Christmas
into the New Year,
travel with us.

Christmas Eve

We meet to wait and watch
with Mary and Joseph in the stable,
with shepherds on the hill.

*We meet to praise God
summoned by the heavenly host.*

We meet to worship
with people watching and waiting
throughout the whole world.

We meet to celebrate the coming of Christ
into the world.

The Word was made flesh
and dwelt among us
and we beheld his glory.

Birth

To wait
to endure
to be vulnerable
to accept
to be of good courage
to go on
day after day after day;
to be heavy with hope
to carry the weight of the future
to anticipate with joy
to withdraw with fear
until the pain overcomes,
the waters break
and the light of the world
is crowned.
Then the travail is over,
joy has overcome.

Lord of heaven and earth,
crowned with blood at your birth,
delivered with pain,
bring new hope to birth
in your waiting world,
bring fresh joy
to those who weep.
Be present
in all our dyings and birthings.

Open the stable door

Unto us a child is born.
Unto us a Son is given,
And his Name is called
Prince of Peace.

Loving God, Holy One of Israel,
soon to come to us
in Bethlehem, least of cities,
we offer you praise,
and hearts lifted high,
for in the communion of your love
Christ comes close to us,
and we come close to Christ.

O God, bring new life
where we are worn and tired,
new love where we have turned hard-hearted,
forgiveness where we have wounded,
and the joy and freedom of your Holy Spirit
where we are prisoners of ourselves.

(Silence)

So let us open the stable door
and kneel with shepherds and cattle.
Let us ponder the Word made flesh.
Let us glory in our Saviour,
and then having received the living Lord
in our hands
let us go on our way rejoicing.

Cords of love

Mary sits,

> the child rocked in her womb
> now rocked in her arms.

Joseph stands

> the child given to him
> now bound to his heart.

We kneel

> the child come to us
> now capturing our love.

O God, come to us once more,
bind us to you
with cords of love.
Lead us with reins of kindness
and bring us to fullness of life.

Draw us onwards

O God,
houses and trees, buses and shops
are silhouetted against a dark blue sky.
As the lights of the town beckon,
may your star of promise
draw us onward and nearer our destination:
to know more deeply who and where we are,
to worship you and glorify your name for ever;
through the Christ-child of Bethlehem,
Crucified God, we ask this.

Son bright

Almighty One,
who brought us through the darkness of sleep
to the bright light of a new day,
guide us through this year:
in dark and light,
in pain and joy,
in snow and sunshine,
through heartbreak to sonbright
and from today's joyous light
bring us to the guiding light of eternity.

At the gate of the year
strengthen those
who look back through tears
and forward without hope.
Covenant with those who trust in you.

Holy Spirit, giver of new life
open our mouths in praise,
our hearts to welcome the Christ-child
and our arms to embrace the world.

Snowmoon

The moon is caught in the ash tree
and snow is on its way.
Cold and grey are the waves of the sea
and snow is on its way.
I see the moon and feel the spray,
I smell the snow and smile.
Winter's reign is almost over,
the solstice will turn the tide.

Time turns

Clocks tick
time turns
bells chime
the new year
sweeps across the world
in glory.

Glory to you
God of history
and new beginnings.
Glory to you
Lord of eternity.
May we use your gift
of time
more carefully
more prayerfully
more peacefully
from now on
and for ever
Amen.

Unfreeze

Locked in white,
frozen to the marrow,
despairing of spring,
still we come to you, O God.

You are in the snow;
you are in the cold;
you secretly nourish growth

and plan the surprise
  of snowdrop and daffodil.
Melt our frozen hearts, Lord;
  help us forgive.
Unlock our frozen minds, Lord;
  help us accept forgiveness.

Winter solstice

Small birds,
blowing like ash on the wind,
prepare to leave,
as nights draw in
and days are short.

Small children,
bouncing like corks on water,
prepare for parties,
as tempers fray
and tasks mount up.

But the darkest and coldest time
is also the brightest time:

O Christmas Christ,
the radiance around the moon
is not as fair
as the radiance
around your head.

O holy one,
the majesty of the winter sea
is not as glorious
as your majesty.

At the departing times,
the coldest times
of our lives;
at the times of excitement
and the times of expectancy,
at the times of intersection,
when hard choices
have to be made,
be with us
Prince of Peace.

Grant us warmth,
grant us calm,
grant us hope
in our journey
into a New Year.

Epiphany

Epiphany is a jewel
multifaceted,
flashing colour and light.
Epiphany embraces
the nations of the world,
kneeling on a bare floor
before a child.
Epiphany shows
a man
kneeling in the waters of baptism.
Epiphany reveals
the best is kept for last
as water becomes wine
at the wedding feast.

O Holy One
to whom was given
the gifts of power and prayer,
the gift of suffering,
help us to use
these same gifts
in your way
and in your name.

Far and wide

Open my eyes,
my ears, my mind;
open my imagination
to your presence and your love,
mysterious God.

Open my hands, Lord,
that I may sow with generosity.
Unclench my fists, Lord,
that I may scatter the good news
of your coming
far and wide.

Into Egypt

The bucketing, banging wind is stilled
and the moon is cold and clear.
Castles like candles guard the coast
and the moon is ringed with fire.

> The coble's ashore and the logs are cut
> the moon rides alone in the sky
> until the shivering sliver of light appears:
> the star in the east, the sign of hope,
> rising to claim its place
> in the hearts and the hearths of all the earth
> proclaiming the dawn of peace.

Open your hearts and your homes tonight.
Welcome the dawn of hope;
throw wide the arms of your love today,
embrace the dawn of love.

Then the freezing wind returns,
the sky is streaked with black.
The glory is gone,
the hills remain,
distant and coldly white.
The sea retreats,
the castles stand
and the moon is hidden from sight.
The child is restless,
the refugee cold,
the mother afraid once more.

Then is the time to know it's true.
Then is the time to cling to hope.
Then is the time to pray for love:
when it's dark and cold
and hope is scarce;
when it's windy and wet and sad.
Then is the time to hope for faith
in a world the Creator made.

So open your hearts and your homes tonight,
throw wide the arms of your pain;
against all the odds
despite all the hurt
risk the piercings of the wind,
risk the demands of love.

Not for the faint-hearted

Lent is not for the faint-hearted

Lent is not for the faint-hearted.
It demands that we, like Thomas,
put our hand into the side of the crucified Christ.

Lent is a journey towards the cross,
a journey of enlightenment:
from wilderness to feast,
from desert to oasis.
It's an attempt to identify with the powerless
and the suffering in the world.

Lent is not tidy.
The days grow longer,*
the ground thaws, there's mud and dirt everywhere
and the windows need cleaning.

Lent is a journey.
So at the end of Lent
we should expect to find ourselves
somewhere different from where we started.

Lent can be an opportunity
to explore what is the nature
of the promised Kingdom of God on earth
that we long for;
a time to discern
how we are called to work for it.

No, Lent is not for the faint-hearted!

*'Lent' means lengthen.

Promise of Spring

Pale winter sun,
flooding the earth
with your light,
gilding the bare trees
with your touch.
Your eyes
have seen
the glory
of the Lord.

Low white candles of hope
palely gleaming in the dark earth,
your advent heralds
the promise of Spring;
your green hearts
speak of God's renewing love.

Son of God,
show us the way.
Light our path.
Lead us
through this Lenten desert
to Easter with you
beyond the pain
of loss and fear.
Lead us in new ways
of trusting service.

A green heart

Into a dark world
a snowdrop comes,
a benison
of hope and peace,
carrying within it
a green heart,
symbol of God's renewing love.

Come to inhabit our darkness
Lord Christ,
for dark and light
are alike to you.

May nature's white candles of hope
remind us of your birth
and light our journey
through Lent and beyond.

Kingdom light

The people that walked in darkness
have seen a great light.
They that dwell in the shadows,
have come out into the day.
The Lord is my light,
my light and my salvation.

Praise to the God of the desert;
Praise to the God of the marketplace;
Praise to the God of the seashore,
for Christ driven by the Spirit,
for Christ empowered in the wilderness,
for Christ at work in the city.

Holy Spirit of saving power,
in repentance we turn to you,
setting aside all that imprisons us.
In your power may the yoke of injustice
be lifted from the backs of the poor.
As the small and unrecognised
are brought to light,
may we proclaim you boldly
and live faithfully and unashamed
in the glorious light of your kingdom.

God, fill us with your fullness.
God, shield us with your shade.
God, fill us with your grace,
that for the sake of your anointed Son
we may be his eyes and hands and feet
in your world.

Knock and open

As buds uncurl
and flowers open their faces to the sun,
turn us
to the light and warmth
of your presence,
that in confidence
we may confess our sin

(Silence)

God of justice, peace and love,
we knock at your gate
with our prayers:
we confess that our lives
and the life of the world
are broken apart
by our sin.

Lord have mercy,
Christ have mercy,
Lord have mercy.

As we open the door to justice,
       we ask to be forgiven.
As we open the door to peace,
       we ask to be renewed.
As we open the door to love,
       we ask to be made whole.

Show me the path that leads to life

Down here in the forest of terror,
down here in the undergrowth of fear
each heartbeat echoes,
each thought flies blindly
like a bird trapped in a room.
Down here, dodging panic,
listening to each twitch and thump of my body,
down here life is not worth living.

So what if I find a snowdrop
or a ray of sunshine penetrates the darkness?
What if it's true that darkness
and light are alike to you;
that Christ has harrowed hell?

O, make it true,
turn the clock,
rescue me, O Lord.
Show me the path
that leads to life.

You are there

If I travel through the desert
you are there.
If all my thoughts are arid
you are there.
If all of life seems pointless
and throws you on the scrapheap
you are there … and there … and there.

For all my fears and feverings,
all my anguish,
all my hollowness,
all the haunted conversations
in my head
cannot erase your beauty
or take away your faithfulness.

You are there
and here
and always.
You are there
immovable,
immutable;
you are here.

Like a drowning person clutching a straw
or a scream running across a bridge
I cling to hope
and run towards
the arms of God
to welcome me home.

You are there.

Lent darkness

*Dragons lurk in desert spaces
penetrating the mind with evil claw.
Serpents' teeth seek out the chinks
insidiously, relentlessly gnawing on the bone;
searching out the interstices of muscle and sinew.*

*Such is the pain of the wilderness.
Alone, alone, alone*

Christ sits
in the waste place of abandoned pleas and questions
until exhausted.
Finally
at last
the realisation
comes
that in the end
there is only
God.

In the night-time of our fears
and in our time of questioning,
be present, ever present God.
Be present with those
camped out in the fields of hopelessness,
with refugees and the homeless,
those who live lives of quiet desperation.
Be present until the desert places
blossom like the rose
and hope is born again.

Mothering

Come, Mother God,
come as an enfolding
nurturing presence;
Come as steadfast love
    to hold us.

Come, Mother God,
come as an enabling
strengthening force;
Come as tough love
    to let us go.

Come, Mother God,
come as friend and comforter
healing our wounds,
walking our way;
Come as wounded healer
    to make us whole.

Christ our true mother,
you have carried us
within you,
laboured with us
and brought us forth to bliss.
Enclose us in your care
that in stumbling
we may not fall,
nor be overcome by evil,
but know that all shall be well.

Thanksgiving

For the mothering of mothers
and the mothering of fathers;
for the mothering of others:

Mother God,
we give you thanks.

For those who act as midwife
to our hopes,
for those who nurse us through our pain,
for those who nurture, strengthen and guide us:

Mother God,
we give you thanks.

For those who gently push us from the nest,
for those who welcome us home,
for those who become our family,
for the motherhood of the Church:

Mother God,
we give you thanks.

Commitment

O Christ our true mother,

To Mothering:
>   to cradling and to nurturing,
>   to holding and to letting go,

>   *We commit ourselves*
>   *as your community*
>   *in this place.*

To Mothering:
>   to comforting and to challenging,
>   to forgiving and to releasing,

>   *We commit ourselves*
>   *as your community*
>   *in this place.*

To Mothering:
>   to laughter and to friendship,
>   to hospitality and to mission,

>   *We commit ourselves*
>   *as your community*
>   *in this place.*

Kindred

My heart looked up and saw you.
My mind leapt forward to embrace.
My feet ran to meet you,
as your arms stretched out to me.

God, our Lover,
as husbands and wives,
friends and partners
grow through their love,
learn by their mistakes,
are united yet separate,
so may we be dependent on you,
be independent of you,
be interdependent with you,
that we may truly be
Mother, Brother and Sister of Christ,
one kindred,
one household of faith.

Let us cling to you.
Let us let go.
Let us make love
our pattern and goal.

Christ, our Brother,
loose the bonds
that bind us to the past,
the cords that strangle;
bring us to a new relationship
where duty is delight,
carers are cared for
and all may live freely
in your Kingdom of peace.

Penitence

God, love-giver,
the love that dares to speak out,
the love that listens,
the love found most powerfully in weakness,
the love that heals;
this is the love we need and long for,
not counterfeit pretty love, tied with bows,
but lasting love:
love that's there when the sweetness has gone:
love that endures beyond the barrier of pain.

Forgive us
for worshipping the idols of perfection,
for failing to see your glory in the vulnerable,
for attaching more worth to the seen
than the unseen:

> *Lord have mercy,*
> *Christ have mercy.*

Forgive us
for being so full of our own importance
that we cannot do the one thing needful:

> *Lord have mercy,*
> *Christ have mercy.*

Forgive us
our lack of perseverance
in the face of failure, doubt, rejection;
our failure to make connections
between politics and health,
economics and healing:

> *Lord have mercy,*
> *Christ have mercy.*

Vulnerable Love-giver,
Christ, wounded healer,
Holy Spirit, compassionate friend,
grant us love in all its fullness.

Wrapped in God's love

Wrapped in the arms of God's love,
as a child wrapped in a shawl;
fed from God's very being,
as a child nourished at the breast;
resting on the knees of God's love,
as a child leans against the teacher;

let us pray

for all communities destroyed by monetary policies
    which sacrifice society to individual greed;
for all organisations imprisoned by economic policies
    which sacrifice compassion to market forces;
for all countries ruined by their debt to us
    which makes nonsense of our aid to them.

Mother of infinite wisdom,
Christ of infinite compassion,
Holy Spirit, guarantor of change,
bring us to our knees in shame,
bring us to our feet in action,
bring us to our senses in prayer,
that with you we may all inherit
a new heaven and a new earth.

Steadfast love

Gracious God,
for your love for us,
gentle as a shower,
healing our pain,
binding our wounds,
we give you thanks.

For your love for us,
sure as the dawn,
transforming our darkness,
revealing your truth,
we give you thanks.

For your love for us,
mercifully steadfast,
calling us to you,
raising us up,
we give you thanks.

For your love for us,
encouraging questions,
open to doubts,
making us vulnerable,
we give you thanks.

Urge us on, O Christ,
to find wholeness
through serving you
by serving others,
in the power of your Spirit.

Choices

God of the heights and the depths,
we bring to you
those driven into the desert,
those struggling with difficult decisions.

May they choose life.

God of the light and the darkness,
we bring to you
those lost in the mist of drugs or drink,
those dazzled by the use of power.

May they choose life.

God of the wild beast and the ministering angel,
we bring to you
those savaged by others' greed,
those exhausted by caring for others.

May they feel your healing touch.

Christ tempted and triumphant,
we bring ourselves to you,
tired of difficult choices,
anxious about the future,
drained by the loss of a loved one.

May we feel your healing touch.

May we feel your healing touch,
know God's presence in all things
and receive the crown of life
through the Holy Spirit of compassion.

Flower fragrance

Green-hearted winter snowdrop,
symbol of God's renewing love,
turn your face to the sun,
as the days lengthen
and he sets his face to go to Jerusalem.

Pale yellow hosanna trumpet of spring,
accompany him on his journey,
and as your shining petals brighten our day,
help us to sense his presence in our darkness,
his suffering in the agony of the world.

Flower fragrance of anointed love,
fill our house, our hearts, our world,
with the life-giving news of Easter.

Palm – Passion

Partisan God,

taking sides with life against death;
conqueror on the back of a donkey,
you carry with you
the expectations of the centuries.
You are shoot of Jesse, descendant of David,
offspring of Moabite Ruth gleaning in alien corn.
You are master carpenter, compassionate healer.
You are the one we are waiting for.

Christ of vinegar and gall,

help us to learn to die in freedom from fear.
Show us the lengths to which God's love will go.
Save us from our godless self-contempt.
Reawaken in us the song of protest.
Remind us that our sisters and brothers starve.
Enable us to comfort the empty and feed the hungry.
Call us to release the captives waiting in hope,
and through your costly love
bring us to a deeper understanding
of the meaning of suffering.

Holy Spirit of struggle,

as we grapple with your struggle and ours,
'as blind we sit in the tomb you raised us from'*
grant us your blessing.

*Gerard Manley Hopkins

Cross-carrying Jesus

Cross-carrying Jesus,
as you stagger on your lonely journey
time slips,
worlds reel.

Forgive us that we turn away
embarrassed
uncaring
despairing.

Help us to stay with you through the dark night
to watch and wait,
to know the depths of your anguish
and to realise that you carry us,
forgive (even) us
and love us.

Forgive us
that we get on with our work unthinking,
that we gamble unknowing with precious things.

Cross-carrying Jesus,
nailed to the tree of life,
forgive us
and grant us your salvation.

The garden

Christ
    spread-eagled
    across the tilting earth
    hands clutching
    dead leaves;
Christ
    grappling
    groaning
    overwhelmed
    clinging
    to the sweet spring flowers;

Christ
    heartbroken
    alone
    handed over to our decisions,
    while the moon
    slides behind a cloud
    in fear,
    the stars hang their heads

in shame
and no bird sings;
does anyone
cling to a weeping tree
mingling tears
in that dark wood
on that dark night,

while we
seek the denial
of sleep,
avoid anguish
too deep to bear?

Now we,
thank God,
need not
go into
that dark night
alone.

God's Friday

Anointed
for burial
with gentle kisses,
nothing
nothing
nothing
prepared him for this:
the thud of hammers,
nails biting into
his wrists,
his feet;
the lurch
as his body
swung forward
and down
into the pit
of despair;
the godforsakenness
breaking
his heart.

How long, O God,
how long, must I endure
this birthing death
until the waters break
and the at-one-ment
is delivered?

'On a pastoral forehead of Wales'*

A rabbit sits entranced
in Hopkins' land.
Everywhere I turn
God's glory burns:
crushed garlic underfoot
an unrepentant song bird
soft swoop of bat
evening sun red-ribbons to rest
and patchwork fields yield to sleep,
as the moon shines on a sad Christ
contemplating his heart
in stony isolation.

Like Mary
I want to hug him
and weep for a sad world.
Has he forgotten his Easter?
Have we forgotten his Easter?
Christ's heart bleeds
and will bleed until …

*The title is taken from Gerard Manley Hopkins' poem
'The wreck of the Deutschland', stanza 24.

Cup of suffering

God of birthing,
God of death,
God of ever-present breath,
God of steadfast faithful love,
God in Christ in borrowed stall,
God in child so weak and small,
    hear us as we pray:

    for those who bear heavy losses,
    for children at risk,

for those camped out
in fields of despair,
for those without work.

Lord hear us,
Lord graciously hear us.

God, mother, midwife, judge,
housewife, shepherd, father, friend,
knee-scarred king on throne of wood,
man of sorrows in borrowed grave,
gardener, stranger on the road,
hear us as we pray:

for those who drink the cup of suffering,
for those who watch over the sick,
for those who proclaim the mystery
of your risen glory.

Lord hear us,
Lord graciously hear us.

God of birthing, God of death,
God of life beyond the grave,
hold out the cup of salvation,
to those who serve your needy world.
Save us from tricking ourselves
into thinking that we are called
to privilege rather than service.

May the man of sorrows,
the crucified Christ,
struggle with us.
As we wrestle with our demons,
may the glorified Christ
enter our pain,
that we may receive a blessing
in the morning.

Sun garden

O God hanged on a tree,
hear our prayer of confession:

In a world of need
   we are but poor clattering cymbals.
In a world of distress,
   we are but dull sounding gongs.
However good we are at liberation theology,
   however many petitions we sign,
without love and understanding
   we are nothing.

Help us to see the connections in our world:
   the brokenness of structures,
   the fragmentation of community,
   the disintegration of self.

When we forget that you are deep in the earth,
   you pervade the air around us,
   you are the bread broken and the wine poured;
when we forget that you are in the shy smile of a child,
   the greeting of a friend;

Help us to see you in the prisoner,
   in the mother who shares her last bowl of rice;
Help us to see you in the other:
     the other side of the argument,
     the other side of the fence,
     the other side of ourselves.

       and seeing you and hearing you
       may we embrace you with joy
       in the sun garden of your love.

The cemetery

In the morning mist I'm sent
to recall the God who calls me by name,
to consider the flowers of the field.

In the midst of glory – danger;
In the midst of beauty – fear:

two dogs appear.
Pit Bull or not
I turn and find another path,
a path through upland meadow
to the Chapel on the Rock.

The mist swirls nearer.
I turn aside to where
'Orate pro anima',
the priests sleep silent,
twin-bunked
in serried rows
and a spade rests against the hedge
waiting for the next ...
as a lamb bleats on the hill
and Christ droops on the cross.

Interlocking circles

A tree falls in Brazil
a child coughs in Sweden
a young man finds work somewhere
a young woman is blown up by a land mine somewhere else.

Interconnecting,
interlocking circles,
cause and effect,
the ripples of our actions
flood the universe.

Gulf War syndrome,
leukaemia clusters,
powdered baby milk
  made up with contaminated water,
all instances of the ripple effect
in a global village.

O God, three persons
  in perfect community,
help us to own the results of our actions,
help us to see the effects of our misuse of matter,
help us to heal the wounds of your world
through the power of love crucified.

Dawn's ribbon of glory

Into living hope
(1 Pet.1:3)

With Peter and the other disciples
who came in haste
and left believing:
Glory and praise to God.

With Mary of Magdala
who stayed to weep
and saw the Lord:
Glory and praise to God.

With all the people of God
who have come in sorrow
and found their joy fulfilled:
Glory and praise to God.

Glory and praise to God,
For Christ has been raised;
Life has conquered death;
Hope has conquered fear.

When Christ our life is revealed,
We will share his glory.

Easter blessing

How beautiful is the blossom
spilling from the tree,
the hidden primrose
and the bluebell
ringing out the news.
He is risen
he is alive
we shall live
for evermore.
The dark winter is past,
the slow, cold, foggy days are over.

May the warmth of your resurrection
touch our hearts and minds
as the warmth of the sun
blesses our bodies.

Easter joy

Christ is risen!
He is risen indeed!

The Sun,
the eye of the great God,
the eye of the king of hosts
is rising upon us,
gently and generously.
Welcome, glorious Son,
dawn of a new day.

Christ is risen
He is risen indeed!

Glory to you, Son of the most high,
human face of God,
labouring with us,
spending your life for us,
cross-bound to set us free.

Christ is risen!
He is risen indeed!

Living One,
sword bright,
first and last,
banish all fear
from our hearts and minds.
Forgive us our sin.
On each of our dyings
shed your lovely light.

Christ is risen!
He is risen indeed!

Bright face of God,
warmed by your glory,

may we run with joy to tell the others
as you go ahead of us
into the world.

Christ is risen!
He is risen indeed!

Skylark and hawk

Tingling dawn freshness,
shock of wet dew grass,
skylark bursting from the ground
to sing, to sing, to sing:
He is risen, risen, risen.

Anguished and weary,
frightened and bold,
deaf to God's message
we come to the tomb.
Empty and broken,
stolen and lost,
robbed of our grieving,
deprived of our host.

Scattered and running
we fall in despair,
a stranger, we mistake him,
fall into his arms,
until he with tenderness,
calling our name,
turns us round firmly
and sets us in flight.

Like hawk from the fist
of the falconer
we soar
to tell all the world:
He is risen indeed!

Touch

The rough bark
pressed against
my forehead
as I clung
to the tree
and let
grief's healing tears
flow.

The strong support
of His forearms
under mine
as He said:
'Don't cling.
Go and tell
the others.'

The wet grass
on my feet
as I flew ...

The warm touch of their hands
as we shared the good news;
the light of Christ shining from our eyes.

All shall cry glory

'The night, the darkness and its mist
have wrapped the world in heavy clouds.
They take to flight as light returns
*and Christ comes now to bless the day.'**

O God, you formed the elements,
the water, fire, the earth and air,
assigning each their work and place
that they may praise you everywhere.
We join with them to praise you
that Christ is risen.

*5th Century hymn

Iona Easter

Speedwell-studded
rainwashed grass
a froth of blue
in a sea of green.
Black islands
floating on a silver mirror.
Twin lambs vulnerable;
protective mother.
Air crisp, cool,
lark caressing;
a butterfly rests
on an abbey buttress.
Gull and dove voices
mingle with the clatter
and tang of the mower.
Easter Iona
when daffodils dance
and the tourists are few.

Adoration

A familiar figure on a distant shore,
a familiar action at a kitchen table,
a presence in the midst of doubt,
O Risen Christ
you come to surprise us and delight us,
you open wide the door to joy;
hopeful, we worship you;
hesitant, we adore.

As the dry stane walls
enfold the fields,
enfold us, O God.

As the becks encircle
the houses,
encircle us, O God.

As the sound of the curlew
and the sight of an Easter lamb
call us to prayer,
encompass us about,
O Lamb of God,
Christ our risen king.

Lord of the morning

Bless to us, O God – this day fresh made.
In the chorus of birds – bless us.
In the scent of blossom – bless us.
In the wet grass and the spring flowers – bless us.
Bless us and heal us,
for we come to you in love and in trust.
We come to you in expectant hope:

(Silence)

O God, give us a well of tears
to wash away the hurts of our lives.
O God, give us a well of tears
to cleanse the wounds,
to bathe the battered face
of our world.
O God, give us a well of tears
or we are left, like arid earth,
unsanctified.

(Silence)

Heal us and your grieving world
of all that harms us.
By the power of your resurrection
restore us to new life,
set us on new paths,
bring us from darkness to light,
help us to choose hope.

Jesus says, 'Pick up your bed and walk,' so:
pick up the bed of your sorrows and fears,
pick up the bed of your grief and your sin,
pick up your life and come, come follow him.

Confession

Lord of the morning,
we come in shame and in fear.
Our lives are imprisoned by false expectations.
We have walled ourselves up
with lies and half-truths.
We are trapped, fearful and ashamed.

Who will roll the stone away?

Lord of Creation,
we come in shame and in despair.
The delicate balance of your creation
has been destroyed.
The fragile face of the earth is mutilated.
We are trapped by the demands of our greed.

Who will roll the stone away?

The God who walked in the garden,
The Christ mistaken for a gardener,
The Spirit who nurtures growth,
will roll away the stones
that choke the life of the planet.
The three in one
will roll away the boulders
that imprison us in guilt.

When we, grieving, confess;
when we, forgiven,
work for truth and peace:

God will release us
from the tomb
of our despair.

Supplication

Look for us Lord.
We are on the edge,
vulnerable and afraid.

> Search for us Lord.
> We are beyond the pale,
> lonely and fearful.

Find us, Lord.
We have wandered far from home,
isolated and rejected.

> *I, your God,*
> *like a good shepherd*
> *have known you*
> *from the beginning of your time.*

> *I hear your cry.*
> *I run to meet you,*
> *as you re-turn to me.*

The tree of defeat
has become the tree of glory.
Where life was lost
life has been restored.

> *Christ is risen!*
> *He is risen indeed!*

Blossom into life

Easter with us, bountiful God,
save your people
from the consequences of their sin.
Where there is division, create unity.
Strike the shackles of oppression
from the empty hands of the poor.
Mend the tapestry of community,
torn by our neglect.

Rise within our concrete jungles
and isolated communities,
that we may blossom into life,
sense hope where full employment
is a long-forgotten dream,
and live to proclaim your victory
in the power of the Holy Spirit.

Thomas

Put your hand,
Thomas,
on the crawling head
of a child,
imprisoned
in a cot
in Romania.

Place your finger,
Thomas,
on the list of those
who have disappeared
in Chile.

Stroke the cheek,
Thomas,
of the little girl
sold into prostitution
in Thailand.

Touch, Thomas,
the gaping wounds
of my world.

Feel, Thomas,
the primal wound
of my people.

Reach out your hands,
Thomas,
and place them at the side of the poor.

Grasp my hands, Thomas,
and believe.

Thanksgiving

Risen Christ,
for recognising you
in the scriptures;
for recognising you
in the breaking of the bread;
for finding you in the stranger:

we give you thanks.

Risen Christ,
for times of doubt and struggle,
for times of confusion and chaos,
for times of wrestling for a blessing:

we give you thanks.

For thankfully
you are present
in bread and in battle,
in darkness and in doubt,
in every corner of our lives,
in every place in our world,
for you have gone before us.

Send us out
with thankful hearts
to live and work
in your name
and to your glory.

Commitment

To you, O God,
who has led us out of captivity,
through the wilderness,
into the garden of Gethsemane
and to the cross,
we cling.

To you, O God,
who has led us out of captivity,
through the wilderness,
into the garden of burial
and to an empty tomb,
we cling.

O Risen Christ,
unclasp our clinging hands.
Turn us from death to life,
and as we commit ourselves
anew to you,
send us out
to tell others
the good news
of your Easter.

Signs of life

Risen Christ,
as ice melts and rivers flow
when spring comes,
breathe your life-giving Spirit
into our frozen hearts.
Set our minds on fire
and our feet running,
to seek and to serve your truth.
Free us from all that captivates us.
Give us a deeper understanding of your truth.
Increase our wisdom.
Remind us that you have written our names
on the palms of your crucified hands
and help us to know that you call us by name.

As the heralds of spring
golden trumpet
the arrival of Easter;
as the dark night of Lent passes
and the days lengthen,
so like Cuthbert,
bright star of the north,
we would become
your Easter people, O Christ,
shepherds of your sheep,
peacemakers and hospitality-givers
open to change and partnership,
Spirit-led, in solitude and costly service.

Transfiguration

O Holy One,
  whose glory shines from the face of your Son,
O Christ, whose glory reflects the image of God,
O Spirit, whose glory transforms our fear,
unveil the fire of your love,
declare the truth of your presence,
      that we, seeing you, may worship you
      and so proclaim Christ as Lord
      and ourselves as his servants.

Christ our light,
  hear us as we pray for your world:
  shrouded in a cloud of famine, war and pollution,
  tainted and deformed by grim deceit.

    Bring healing.
    Bring peace.

Christ our friend,
  hear us as we pray for ourselves:
  for clarity about the future,
  for sensitivity in our relationships,
  for courage to face tomorrow,
  as we explore on the plain
  the implications of the mountain top.

    Bring healing.
    Bring peace.

Holy Spirit of Truth, devouring fire of love:
  may we declare the truth openly,
  burn for God without being consumed,
  be prepared to move and be moved,
  be witnesses of Christ's glory,
  until the day dawns
  and the morning star rises in our hearts.

Ascension sideways

Almighty God,
you are no scarecrow,
fit only to scare the birds in the cucumber fields.
You are a living God,
an everlasting King,
a gentle, caring Mother God,
a patient, loving Father God,
the God of all places and people.
God in everything,
you have pitched your tent among us.

Be present with us now.

Immanuel, God with us:
baby gently nestling,
child courageously seeking,
young man desert-empowered,
healer, teacher, friend,
    as you befriended the poor,
    as you blessed the children,
    as you comforted the sorrowful,
    as you challenged the proud,

Be present with us now.

Christ, crucified and risen
to ascend sideways into the world,
clothe us with power to work in the city.
Equip us for mission.
Gift us with insight.
Grant us compassion.
Steel us to challenge.

Be present with us now.

God hanged on a tree,
descended to lead the captives free,
ascended to fill all things,
in the power of your Spirit
be present with us now
and lead us out into your world.

Pentecost

Come Holy Spirit,
come fire of love,
warm the earth with your touch,
cleanse the polluted waters of creation,
restore balance,
bring healing,
pour out energy,
lighten skies
darkened by our sin.

Come Holy Spirit,
come renewer of life,
nourish the potential in us all.
In our work and in our leisure
waken us to fresh opportunities.
In our families and community life
nurture and inspire our creativity
in all things.

Come Holy Spirit,
come wind of God,
whisper your tender words of healing
in the ears of the sick,
breathe your spirit of comfort
around those who mourn,
stir hearts hardened by despair
to new life and hope.

Drive us out of our pious ghettos
to glimpse new ways to witness,
new ways to use our wealth,
new ways to work for peace,
new ways of being the people
you call us to be.

Come Holy Spirit
Renew the whole creation.

Invocation

Come Holy Spirit,
come as the robin in the morning,
awakening our hearts
with your song.

Come as the dove at evening,
bringing blessing and peace.

Come as the blackbird at noonday,
gladdening your world with joy.

Come to us
as we come to worship,
that we may
sing to the Creator,
grapple with the wounds of creation
and find peace
through active prayer.

Come

Holy Spirit,
come like a mother
to tend the wounds of a hurting world.
Come like a lover
to inspire the unloved.
Come like a worker
to labour for justice and peace.
Come like a child
to open our eyes to God's love.
Come like a sister
to support us in our need.
Come with power and tenderness
to rule our hearts.

Forgive

God of all mercy
your forgiveness and compassion
call forth within us
songs that fill our hearts
with gladness.

> As the waves gather, pause and fall,
> so does the ongoing work of the Spirit
> ebb and flow:
> relentless, gentle, powerful,
> cleansing the beach of rubbish,
> washing away the debris of life,
> soothing the heart with her song;
> forgiving all that is past,
> preparing the way for the future.

So, merciful God,
may we show mercy
to those who betray us,
forgiveness to those who wound.
As you have pitied us,
and raised us in your arms,
so may we be reconciled
to those who hurt us.

By the power of your Spirit
turn us from evil to good.
Keep us in your ways
of righteousness and love,
through Jesus Christ.

Basketful

Spirit of God,
brooding over the waters
of our chaos,
inspire us to
generous living.

Wind of God,
dancing over the desert
of our reluctance,
lead us to the oasis
of celebration.

Breath of God,
inspiring communication
among strangers,
make us channels
of your peace,

that we may give
in deep thankfulness,
placing the overflowing basket
of our gifts
on the table
of rejoicing.

Intercession

Wind of God,
blowing from the four corners of the earth,
breathe on us;
our bones are dried up and our hope is lost.
Breathe hope and sinew into our desperate spirits.
In flooded village,
in refugee camp,
in hungry homes,
may your arm be under the head of the helpless,
may they rise up from the graveyard of despair,
and find new life through the power of love.

Hurricane of God,
blowing across the universe,
stir the hearts of the compassionate,
overturn the caution of the hesitant,
that the resources of the world
may be shared with the hungry,
that tanks may be turned into tractors,
and the debt of millions cancelled.

Breath of God,
gently whispering in our ears,
remove the dust of apathy
which clouds our vision.
Energise us
that we may be
a source of comfort for the sick,
a solace for the bereaved.
Holy Spirit of comfort and change,
send us out in confidence and joy
to keep the faith and share it.

The shadow of the dove*

When dawn's ribbon of glory around the world returns
and the earth emerges from sleep –

The shadow of the dove is seen
as she flies across moor and city.

Over the warm breast of the earth she skims,
her shadow falling on
the watcher in the tower,
the refugee in the ditch,
the weary soldier at the gate.

The shadow of peace
falls across the all-night sitting of a council,
across the tense negotiators
around a table.

The shadow of hope
is cast across the bars of a hostage cell
filling with momentary light
rooms tense with conflict,
bringing a brief respite,
a sliver of gold across the dark.

She flies untiring
across flooded fields,
across a city divided by hate and fear,
across a town wreathed in smoke.

The shadow of reconciliation,
the dove of peace
with healing in her wings,
is felt and seen and turned towards
as she makes righteousness shine
like the dawn,
the justice of her cause
like the noonday sun.

Holy Spirit of love,
bring healing, bring peace.

*Written after seeing a dove banner in Brechin Cathedral.

Together on pilgrimage

Rainbow God

Creator of rainbows,
come through the closed doors
of our emotions, mind and imagination;
come alongside us as we walk,
come to us at work and worship,
come to our meetings and councils,
come and call us by name,
call us to pilgrimage.

(*Silence*)

Wounded healer,
out of our disunity
may we be re-membered;
out of the pain of our division
may we see your glory.
Call us from present
preoccupation
to future community.

(*Silence*)

Spirit of Unity,
challenge our preconceptions,
enable us to grow in love and understanding,
accompany us on our journey together,
that we may go out with confidence
into your world as a new creation –
one body in you,
that the world may believe.

Confession for Aidantide

Pilgrim God, how slow we are to follow in the footsteps of Aidan.
Forgive us our laziness, our reluctance to read and study the scriptures.
Where Aidan was humble and loving
we have been proud.

Lord have mercy;
Christ have mercy.

Humble Christ, how slow we are to walk alongside the poor.
Forgive us our busyness, our anxiety to accomplish rather than to listen.

Lord have mercy;
Christ have mercy.

Holy Spirit, freedom-giver, forgive us that we still imprison others
  in our expectations.
Help us ransom those sold into the slavery of greed and addiction.
Where Aidan brought the torch of Christ for all to see, forgive us for
  hiding the light.

Lord have mercy;
Christ have mercy.

Merciful Christ, forgive and free us from all that restrains and diminishes us;
make us whole again, able to live in loving service of you in all people.

Lighten our darkness

When the day's beginning
is dark and grim
Lighten our darkness.
> When my heart thuds
> from one fear to the next
> *Lighten my darkness.*

When the next task
seems insurmountable
Lighten our darkness.
> When my mind races
> like a rat in a trap
> *Lighten my darkness.*

When all seems lost
over the 'cliffs of fall'*
Lighten our darkness.

O encompassing Love
be our shield and our companion.
Calm us as you stilled the storm.
Enfold us in your loving arms.
Encourage us to pilgrim with you
and surround us always
with the halo of your presence.

*Gerard Manley Hopkins

Pilgrimage

Pilgrim God,
our shoes are filled with stones,
our feet are blistered and bleeding,
our faces
are stained with tears.

As we stumble and fall
may we know your presence
in the bleeding and the tears,
and in the healing and the laughter
of our pilgrimage.

Lindisfarne

*Thousands the feet
that cross from mainland to island;
many the prayers
that are said.*

*As the tide ebbs and flows
may the pilgrim's journey be blessed.*

Pilgrim God,

as you welcome us,
may this place be a place of hospitality;
as you call us out,
may this place be a place of challenge;
as you heal and strengthen us
may this place be a place of wholeness;
as you send us out
may this place be a place of departure,

that your love may be shared
wherever we pilgrim.

Following Jesus

'One more step along the world we go.'*
For those whose steps are dogged by fear,
for those whose steps are weak and slow,
we pray, *'Keep them travelling along with you.'*

'One more step along the world we go.'
For those who dare not venture out,
for those who refuse your invitation,
we pray, *'Keep them travelling along with you.'*

'One more step along the world we go.'
For those embittered by life's disappointments,
for those finding solace in forbidden pleasure,
we pray, *'Keep them travelling along with you.'*

'One more step along the world I go.'
For ourselves, fearful, hesitant, tempted, searching,
we pray, *'Keep us travelling along with you.'*

*Italic lines adapted from a hymn by Sydney Carter: One more step along the world I go.

Commitment

Like a thousand springs,
bubbling up
in the well of eternal youth,
the nightingale sings her plaintive song:*

>   Peace to the pilgrim,
>   courage to the searcher,
>   glory to the Lord of the garden.

In the wilderness,
in the common place,
in the heights and depths of our lives,

fill us with hopeful song,
surround us with the sounds of peace,
kindle a flame of courage within us,
that we may continue,
with courage, hope and peace,
the journey that you set before us,
God of all creation.

Written after hearing a nightingale near the Hanta Yo Community, in Surrey.

Between three and six in the morning ...
On reading Matthew 14:22–36

On a black day,
the ferry sets out from Iona,
loaded with pilgrims.
Tumbled and tossed,
it seeks the refuge of the rocks.
Through the mist and rain
time slips, worlds reel,
the horizon bends
and Christ is here –
talking to the boatman!

Lord of the unexpected moment,
Christ the surprising,
why do we always
try to own you,
mistake reality for dream,
shut the door on the impossible?

Calm our fears,
shatter the walls we build
to keep you out.
Confront our hypocrisy.
Catch us when we fail.
Son of God
save us from ourselves.

Blessing the boats*

Holy God,
as you called Noah
to make a boat to rescue your people,
as you parted the Red Sea to let your people pass,
as you rescued Jonah from the belly of the big fish,
as you walked on water and stilled the storm,
as you called fisherfolk from their nets to fish for people,
     rescue us,
       deliver us from our slavery,
       still our fear,
       calm our minds,
       call us to pilgrimage.

Bless those who guard our coast,
those who watch over the waters.
Bless those who wrench a living from the sea
and those who harvest the produce of the deep.

Bless those who offer hospitality
and those who are received as guests.
Bless those who come as sightseers
and continue as pilgrims.

Bless us and this community
and as we cast our bread
on the waters of your creation,
renew us in faith and unity.

We ask this through Jesus Christ
who taught us to pray together: Our Father …

O God, guard those who keep watch
over our coastlines and shores.

The guarding of the God of life be with you.
The guarding of loving Christ be with you.
The guarding of Holy Spirit be with you,
every day of your lives;

to aid you and enfold you,
each day and night of your lives.

*Written for Craster, Northumberland.

Hallowing*

Pilgrim God,
gathered in by your kindness,
we thank you for your steadfast love
which has sustained and fed us on our journey.

We thank you for the different communities working together in this place:
>   for the voices of the kindly,
>   the touch of the compassionate,
>   the laughter of children,
>   the words of the discerning,
>   and for the depth of silence.

For your presence around us in every blessed thing, we thank you:
>   from field to croft,
>   from seashore to machair,
>   in our homes and in our communities,
>   we sense that you are here
>>   to welcome us
>>   to journey with us
>>   alongside us in grief and joy.

But beneath the rose, the thorn,
>   above the mountain, the cloud –
all is not perfect in the garden of your creating.

So we thank you most of all for our brother Jesus,
who in his own body breaks down the walls that divide us.
Through him we bring to you the heavy burden of the world's pain, and our own.

We bring the people and places that are hurting,
>   the rights that need to be restored,
>   and the needs that have not been met.

We confess our share in what is broken;
    our guilt and our shame.
The sea of our complex universe is so large
    and our boat is so small.

        God, have mercy on us:
        Christ have mercy on us.

O God, open to us the oceans of your mercy
    that we may restore and rebuild
        places and relationships;
    that we may heal and be healed.

        God, have mercy on us:
        Christ have mercy on us.

And now give us grace to forgive others
    as you have forgiven us.

        God, have mercy on us:
        Christ have mercy on us.

Holy and compassionate God,
may your Firebright Spirit
    encourage us to dance,
    restore us to community,
    challenge us to campaign for peace with justice
    enable us to live graciously and lovingly
    within the Trinity of your presence,
    One God in perfect Community.

**Written for the Iona Community's annual Hallowing Service, 1999,
when new members are received.*

A pilgrimage prayer from Holy Island

At the going out of the tide
and at its incoming
we will remember them:

pilgrims following in the footsteps of the saints,
missionaries speaking the truth in love,
teachers sharing insights and skills,
hospitality-givers,
silence-seekers;

MAY THEY BE FOUND BY A WELCOMING GOD.

When the sand is revealed,
when the causeway is clear at low tide,
we will remember them:

those who are at a low ebb in their lives,
those seeking a firm path,
those searching for direction;

MAY THEY BE FOUND BY A SEEKING GOD.

At high tide when all is cut off,
we will remember them:

those who see no way out of difficult and hurtful situations;

MAY THEY BE FOUND BY THE CHRIST
WHO IN HIS OWN BODY BROKE DOWN ALL DIVISIONS.

Holy Spirit,
you brood over the waters of our chaos.
As the tide turns, keep us faithful to our vision;
guide our feet into your ways
and our hands to rebuild to your glory:

fill our minds and hearts
with the fire of heavenly love that Cuthbert knew
and grant us wisdom and understanding
of each other;

through the Sacred Three we pray,
One God in Perfect Community.

Thanksgiving

Disturbing stranger,
you call and we follow.
You call, and we leave behind
the nets of our past lives;
the things that bound and held us;
our old selves and our regrets.

For calling and disturbing,
for surprising and making new,
for moving us towards wholeness,
we thank you Lord.

Asylum seekers

Bags packed
ready to go
at a moment's notice.
When is the right time?
Now?
No, hang on a few minutes,
a few days.
Let's not let go all that is dear
and familiar
to venture into the unknown.
Can this house not be our castle
this home our refuge?

The sound of splintering glass;
the phone call in the night;
the friend slipping in the back door;
voices and unknown faces at the front;
cameras and microphones;
can they run as fast as we can?

Someone quietly says:
it's time to go.
Quickly, silently,
round the back hedge,
into the lane and waiting car.
The decision has been taken.
We've cut the mooring rope,
we are adrift in a hostile world,
the stigma of hate and fear
emblazoned on our foreheads.
Where O God shall we find rest
and forgiveness for our souls?

Into God's welcoming arms we flee.

Wisdom is calling

Wisdom is calling us
to cancel debt
to risk in faith
to give
unconditional love.

Wisdom whispers
in the rubbish dumps
of South America;
in the arid wastes
of suburban jungles,
in the brothels
and the desolate home.
Wisdom whispers words of comfort,
words of hope to the evicted and the lonely.
Wisdom reminds us that in a vast universe
God became matter,
that we could be made whole.
God became one of us in Jesus,
who was hungry and homeless,
afraid and betrayed.
He teaches us that when we help those
who are without to find food and shelter
we welcome Him.

Spirit of Wisdom,
breath of God,
awaken in us
understanding and forgiveness
insight and commitment
as we try to follow
in the footsteps
of Jesus.

Eucharist

Holy God,
for the universe you have made
in all its variety and mystery,
we praise and thank you.

For the gift of your Beloved Son,
vulnerable healer,
we praise and thank you.

For your work of salvation,
love crucified and victorious,
we praise and thank you.

With people everywhere,
past, present and yet to come,
we praise and thank you.

That you have brought us together
around this table,
no longer strangers but pilgrims,
companions on a journey,
we praise and thank you.

Send your Spirit of faith, hope and love
on us now and on this bread and wine,
that sharing them
we may become your living body
active in your world.

Address to a pilgrim

Rome to Canterbury
Derry to Iona
Iona to Bamburgh
Bamburgh to Bradwell
Whitby to Whithorn –
Pilgrimage is a circular route,
following the scuffmarks of history.

Beware the onslaught of nostalgia,
look out for sickly sentimentality,
the saintly monk who never broke a fingernail
or into sweat.
Remember, rather, and walk
in the footsteps of countless refugees,
tramping the forests of fear,
camping out in the fields of hopelessness;
the scent, not of crushed myrtle, but panic,
the sound, not of the lark, but of the sniper's bullet,
soaring, seeking warm flesh.

Seek then to remember
the brave steps of Mandela,
the unfinished work of Luther King,
the courage and compassion of Romero.
Carry with you also herstory:
Margaret of Scotland and Hilda of Whitby;
Clothilde and Bertha, persuasive princesses;
Elizabeth Fry and Emily Pankhurst,
who broke open prisons and set free prisoners.

Remember all the invisible ones;
walk in the footmarks of the forgotten ones.

And when your place of departure
becomes also your place of arrival
and you 'know the place for the first time'*
What has changed?
What have you indulged?
In seeking have you been found?
In penance have you travelled
the long hard road to restitution?
And as you step off and out of the procession,
what of you will those who continue
carry until you meet again?
What of them do you bring to us?

* T.S. Eliot

The gentling of friends

God in a box

Creator God of earth and sky,
maker of fresh fields and sun-baked desert,
you threw the stars into space,
you populated the sea with fish,
you fashioned the delicate daisy,
but we continue to restrain you,
to box you in,
to hedge our bets,
to confine you in conditional clauses.
You offer us everything;
we respond with percentages.

Christ wrapped in swaddling bands
and laid in a manger,
we continue to tie you down:
'No cripples or children in the temple …
No shouting in church …
No wheelchairs …',
but you upset our neat categories.
You open the way to ecumenical possibilities;
you make women and children visible;
you create communities of love and promise,
where closed doors and minds
had dwelt before.

Holy Spirit of change,
gentle persuader,
encourage us to live
beyond the security of bricks and laws,
in your open community of hope and love.

Presence

Where do we wait on you,
God of all time and place?
Do we have to stand up and be counted;
proclaim your message, against all the odds?

How do we approach you,
Jesus, priest for ever?
Do we have to bring
costly gifts and promises;
parade our allegiance
for all to see?

At every birthing,
whether it be for death or life,
  Christ is present.

On every torturer's slab,
at every execution,
in every lonely cell,
  Christ is present.

In every mother's heart,
at every mourner's side,
on every helper's hand,
  Christ is present.

Christ is present in the touch of friends.
Christ is present when earth shakes.
Christ is present when floods engulf.
Christ is present when fire burns.

Help us to recognise you,
deep within and all around.
Help us to identify you
in the midst of suffering,
at the heart of suffering,
coming not with answers
but with 'lightening and love';*
a priest for ever
in the kingdom of now.

* Gerard Manley Hopkins

Forgive us

How can we seek the warm safety of worship,
when so many are lonely and afraid?

O loving God,
help us to find worship to be
a sending and strengthening,
not to seek it
as an escape from reality.

> For expecting too much,
> for expecting too little,
> *GOOD LORD, FORGIVE US.*

> For making easy promises
> and failing to keep them,
> *GOOD LORD, FORGIVE US.*

> For hasty words and thoughtless actions,
> for easy answers and careless thinking,
> *GOOD LORD, FORGIVE US.*

> For avoiding the hurt of the world
> and ignoring the needs of others,
> *GOOD LORD, FORGIVE US.*

Those who seek shall find.
Those who ask for forgiveness
are forgiven.

Our failure

O God, make us aware;
help us to understand.
Forgive our acts of discrimination,
whatever they may be.

Forgive us our failure
to hear and understand
the cries of those condemned
because of the colour of their skin
or the shape of their body.

Lord have mercy on us.

Forgive us our failure to hear and understand
those who are discriminated against
at work, at school, at home,
because they look different,
talk with a different voice,
see out of different eyes.

Lord have mercy on us.

O Jesus, forgive us our failure
to hear and understand people
who make us feel uncomfortable.

Lord have mercy on us.

O God, make us more aware;
help us to understand more,
and forgive our acts of discrimination,
whatever they may be;
through Jesus Christ, Lord of all.

Hope

God of all hopefulness:

If we have made gold our hope,
    forgive us.
If we have made success our confidence,
    forgive us.
If we have rejected the cause of the poor,
    forgive us.
If we have rejoiced in the ruin of others,
    forgive us.

For in you alone is our hope.

As you nourished us with hope at the breast,
as you implanted hope in us as we grew,
help us to nourish its growth
in us and in our world.

Creator of hope

Hope as delicate as a spider's web,
strong as a hawser;
hope lively and lovely,
this is what has been
planted in us, and our world,
sometimes nurtured,
grown,
come to flower;
sometimes smashed,
broken,
withered.

Help us,
Creator of Hope,

to recognise its growth,
to secure its planting,
to celebrate its flowering
within our hearts,
and throughout your world.

Choose to hope

Let us choose hope:

jumping ditches
climbing fences
choosing hope;

planning meetings,
preparing dialogue,
choosing hope;

digging wells,
remaking roads,
growing hope;

getting up,
taking nourishment,
choosing hope.

Lord, in a world
of ethnic cleansing,
peace talks,
development and daily living,
when optimism flags,
help us to choose to hope;
help our hope to grow.

Hope within

Hope is a dark elusive child
curled in the womb
cradled in our arms,
hope growing, silently, secretly,
fluttering – putting out soft tentacles;
hope – stretching, stirring.

Hope growing silently, secretly,
swelling,
burgeoning,
bursting,
until the flower opens,
the child is crowned,
and hope is born.

God of all hopefulness,
for seeds of silent growth
and secret expectation,
we thank you.

God of steadfast love,
never leave us hopeless.
Bring hope to birth
in us, and your world.

God, giver of peace,
grow hope within us
and around us.
God of steadfast love,
never leave us hopeless.

Dandelion clock

Hope is a dark elusive child
curled in the womb;
cradled in our arms.
It can be lost,
disappear,
blown on the wind like a dandelion clock.

Its going,
its ebbing away
leaves us
grieving,
empty,
hopeless.

['But' is a hopeful word.]

But,
even as the gossamer
powder-puff
disintegrates,
the seeds are carried
to cling to distant crevices.
As it recedes
it re-seeds
to grow again.

God, giver of peace,
grow hope within and around us.
God of steadfast love,
never leave us hopeless.

Thanksgiving

For the greening of trees
and for the gentling of friends,
we thank you, O God.

For the brightness of field
and the warmth of the sun,
we thank you, O God.

For work to be done
and laughter to share,
we thank you, O God.

We thank you and know
that through struggle and pain
in the slippery path of new birth
hope will be born
and all shall be well.

Christ light

Christ,
light of the world,
illumine us
the unloving,
struggling in the limbo
of unconnected living.
Shed your healing rays
on our brothers and sisters,
whose life blood
seeps into the soil
we stand on.

Spirit of repentance,
enlighten our hearts
to serve our neighbours,
that we may turn back
to face the glorious light
of the face of God.

Storm and tide

The tide is running high,
waves tumultuously
fretting and crashing,
crashing and roaring,
white spume swirling,
powerfully withdrawing,
rushing back in muddy
insidious swirls.

So the tide of humanity:
refugees desperately
running,
noisy warmongers
proclaiming
in accents harsh and clipped,
the power of money
greed and lust,
      defrauding
      abusing
      grabbing.

As you stilled the storm
so long ago, O Christ,
calm our hateful hearts,
stem the tide of our
wanton desires,
halt the march
of invading might.
Bring healing, bring peace.

Children and young people

We affirm the glory of God's creation,
the potential of growth in all people.
We affirm our belief in Christ
as friend and brother.
We affirm the creative energy of the Spirit
awakening goodness,
breaking down barriers.

We commit ourselves
to working with young people;
encouraging their gifts,
enabling their participation,
safeguarding their interests.

We commit ourselves
to supporting each other;
to walking alongside
the doubting and the downcast,
listening, not interfering.

We commit ourselves
to confronting superficial solutions,
speaking not avoiding.

We commit ourselves
to rejoice with those who rejoice,
to weep with those who weep,
to be partners with those who serve.

We commit ourselves –
our time, energy and skills,
in Christ's name, and for his sake.

Intercession*

O God of all youth, we pray to you.
We want to celebrate life,
life before death.
With the hungry and the unemployed,
with the homeless, the oppressed and the sick
we cry out to you.

> Lord in your mercy
> *Hear our prayer.*

Lord of all history,
make new the places ravished by war.
Renew the peoples whose hopes have been destroyed.
Build up communities divided by suspicion.
Reconcile families broken apart by misunderstanding.

> Lord in your mercy
> *Hear our prayer.*

Trinity of love, One God in perfect community,
hear the prayers of your children.
let them come to you,
with all that hurts and disturbs them.
Welcome them with your healing smile.
Encircle them with your strong arms,
and send them out to serve you in the world.

*Adapted from a prayer written by a group of young people from Brazil.

Tools for self-reliance

For the harvesting of anvils
rusting in barns,
Creator God we thank you.

For the singing of sewing machines
put to new use,
Creator God we thank you.

For bobbins and pins
given new life,
Creator God we thank you.

For buckets and pails,
for spanners and hammers,
for forks and for spades
rescued from dusty sheds,
Creator God we thank you.

For the harvest of tools, skills and hope,
Bountiful God we thank you.

For those who give
and those who refurbish
tools for self-reliance;
for those who will receive and use
the harvest not of our fields
but of our past,
Lord of history we thank you.

Alnwick Market Square

For these he came:
busy, friendly market traders,
screeching girls and vacuous boys;
for these he came,
slow moving oldies, with smiles on their faces,
dribbling babies,
haughty ladies,
pensive pensioners;
those whose faces mask
a secret pain,
a silent dread.

For these he came;
for these he is
beside and before,
laughing and joking,
smiling tenderly,
compassionate and perceptive,
just and passionate –

my brother, Jesus.

Christ our Advocate

Christ our Advocate,
we pray for our sisters and brothers throughout the world:
    out of our poverty and theirs,
    may we not stumble
    by judging each other.

Christ, brother of the poor,
in the faces of our partners may we see your love.
    In our faces may they see your love.
    Together may we abide in you,
    celebrating the risen life of the Kingdom.

Christ, bridge-builder,
help us to work with you and for you.
    Through the power of the Spirit
    help us to rebuild God's community of divine purpose
    in partnership with all your people.

Prayer rosary

Hiroshima,
Bosnia,
Belfast,
the names slip through our fingers
like bloodstained beads.

As we tell the story,
tell us,
tell us,
tell us
the way
to peace.

Kosovo,
Afghanistan,
Iraq,

Still they come,
Countless numbers:
people hounded,
refugees tramping the road,
out of hell, into hell.

Where will it stop?
Show us,
show us,
show us
the way to peace.

Five for sorrow,
ten for joy,
may what has been sown in pain
be reaped in hope.

Household of faith

Unless the Lord builds the house
THEY LABOUR IN VAIN THAT BUILD IT.
Unless the Lord keeps the city,
THE WATCHERS WAKE IN VAIN.

O God, key of life,
where our churches lie locked and empty
open us to the possibility of serving you
through serving our community.
FORGIVE US OUR LACK OF VISION.

O Christ, head of the body,
where we lock up the body's treasures
release us to new ways of service,
through the offering of each member's gift.
FORGIVE US OUR LACK OF COURAGE.

O Spirit of God, revealer of truth,
where we fail to recognise you,
create in us an awareness of your presence
in and through the joy and hurt of life.
FORGIVE US OUR LACK OF COMMITMENT.

In the forgiving power of the Spirit
may we rebuild your household of faith
to be Christ's body in the world
and find new life
in an open community
of God's purpose.

Witnesses

Creator God, maker of all,
move within us,
bringing insight and strength,
that we may witness to your saving power
and work with you
to create a new heaven and a new earth.
We stand with you against injustice.

Risen Christ, fulfiller of promises,
raise us to work with you,
that your children
may not be forced to plant
for another to eat,
or bear sons and daughters
to die hungry in their arms.
We stand with you against injustice.

Spirit of Integrity,
inspire us to work
to prevent the rape of the environment,
to safeguard the delicate balance of your creation,
that the whole earth may cry glory
and witness to the victory of Christ.
We stand with you against injustice.

Creating, sustaining, saving God,
make whole your people and your creation,
in the name of the Trinity of Love.

International community

O Christ,
does a mother stop
from stooping and sifting rubbish
in a South American rubbish tip –
    stop and listen to the songbird
    and know that the pain which pierces her heart
    is your pain?

O Christ,
does a child stop
from hustling and haggling with the punters
on the pavements of Brazil –
    stop and look at the stars
    and know that the hunger in his belly
    is your hunger?

O Christ,
does a young girl stop
from walking and working the streets
in the suburbs of the city –
    stop and enjoy the scent of a flower
    and know that the anger in her heart
    is your anger?

O Christ,
does an old man stop
from carrying and cursing the water
in the polluted wastes of Iraq –
    stop and feel the wind on his face
    and know that his thirst
    is your thirst?

Lord, help your Church to hear
your song of praise
in the cry of the hungry and thirsty,
in the despair of the powerless.
And hearing, help us to act justly,
serve wisely and love prayerfully.
In your name and for your sake.

Potter

In the hands of the Potter
the untreasured become the treasured,
the unvalued the valued.
Only speak the word, O Christ,
and we shall be made whole.

Holy Spirit of power,
with your energy
the broken are renewed,
your purposes fulfilled;
so we bring to you
all refugees camped out
in the fields of hopelessness,
all who long to be restored
to health, to their families
and to the church.

Trinity of compassion,
pour your grace
without stint
on those in distress.
Reveal in us your glory,
stir in us your power,
that we may come
from north and south,
from east and west,
to sit at table
in your kingdom of love.

Lawgiver

Marginalised by being different,
marginalised by unjust laws,
marginalised by the forces
of the conqueror,
we cry to you, O Saviour.

Losing the land
which feeds us,
tilling the earth
which another will reap,
driven from the land
to ghetto living,
we cry to you, O Saviour.

Stifled by the confines of culture,
blind to those we make invisible,
deaf to the call of the voiceless,
oppressed by narrow expectations,
limited by lack of vision
and driven by our own need,
we cry to you, O Saviour.

> Lawgiver,
> open to us your shalom.
> By the pruning power
> of your law,
> bring justice to flower,
> compassion to bloom,
> that for the sake
> of your anointed Son,
> we may be his hands and feet
> in your world.

A new dawn

O Jesus, King of the poor,
shield this night
those who are imprisoned without charge,
those who have 'disappeared'.
Cast a halo of your presence round those
who groan in sorrow or pain.

Protect those whose livelihoods are threatened.
Encourage those forbidden to worship.
Encompass your little ones
gone hungry to sleep,
cold and fitfully waking.
Guide your witnesses for peace.
Safeguard your workers for justice.

Encircle us with your power,
encompass us with your grace,
embrace your dying ones,
support your weary ones,
calm your frightened ones –

and as the sun scatters the mist on the hills,
bring us to a new dawn,
when all shall freely sit at table
in your kingdom,
rejoicing in a God who saves his people.

Bread of adversity

Stretch out your arms, O King,
and hear the cry of your people.
Gather us into the company of your faithful.
Though we eat the bread of adversity
and drink the water of affliction,
may we know your presence
and in faith choose to be one with your suffering world.

Stretch out your arms, O Christ,
and bear the pain of your people.
Give bread to a hungry world,
the bread of your body,
broken that we might live.
Feed those who hunger for bread
and those who hunger for justice.

Stretch out your arms, O Spirit,
and uphold those who faint:
your arm under the head of the weary,
your hand to still the restless,
your finger to point the way,
your might to conquer the enemy,
your gentleness to rescue the fearful.

Creator, Saviour, Spirit,
Bread created, broken, shared,
feed us with your love
that we may be manna for the world.

Bread and cup

As bread is broken for the world,
may we feel the world's brokenness.

As we share bread with others,
may we share our time and money.
　　Make us good stewards
　　of what we leave in our pockets,
　　as well as accountable for what we give.
In our common life
may we remember the God of creation,
the mothering, enfolding, naming God,
the God who never abandons us.

As wine is poured out for the world,
may we feel the world's pain.

As we share the cup of suffering
with our neighbour,
may we also share our experience.
　　Make us good stewards of opportunity;
　　to listen, to confront, to work
　　for healing, peace and community.
In our common life
may we remember the God of redemption,
the saving, salving, suffering God;
the God who never forgets us.

Thanks be to God
whose body was broken on a wooden cross
to bring all things into perfect unity,
and to the Spirit whose wings bring healing,
and whose presence spells peace.

A fragment of bread

A fragment of bread
cupped in my hand
torn off from the whole
cupped in my hand
passed to me

And I too must tear the body
to share with my neighbour
a fragment of bread
to embody me with them
and he with us

A piece of bread
a bread of peace
scattered, grown
cut down, mown
gathered, ground
mixed and pummelled
risen, fired and found

A piece of bread
a bread of peace
sliced and toasted
broken, shared
around a table
to give us life.

In the ebb and flow

Wrestle for a blessing

Watch, watch
for the bright shining light in the sky.
Aidan and Hilda have passed through
the gate of glory.

Listen, listen
for the sound of prayer
rippling through the waves.
Cuthbert is knocking at heaven's door.

Sing, sing with Caedmon
the song of God's wonders
in sand, sea and stars.

As Hilda returned to the north
not with joy and praise
but with struggle and reluctance,
so let us wrestle for a blessing,
walk with a limp,
pray with a question,
put our hands in the wounds
of your world, elusive God.

Be aware of the saints
beside and around you:
the keepers of wisdom;
the hospitality givers,
the teachers and healers:
those who shine with the uncreated light of God.

Let all the earth be glad
and the heavens resound
with the delight of God's people.

Spring blessing

God bless to us each sign of spring,
each new green shoot,
each lighter day,
each warmer wind.
God bless to us
rebirth.

The blessing of autumn

As autumn flames across park and field
as smoke curls from ditch and garden,
as birds sing their farewell song,
as frost begins to touch the ground
and our hearts are warmed
by the scent, sound and touch of it;
now is the time to throw away
the heavy stones of anger, regret and fear,
which harden our hearts.
Now is the time to gather stones of praise
to build a cairn
of thankfulness to our God
for all the blessings of our autumn life.

Day and night

O God
bless
the darkness
of the eye
as it lights
on sudden
glory.

Faith

'Prayer is a subversive activity'*

Prayer is subversive.
It changes our minds,
moves mountains,
tumbles walls
and withers fig trees.

Faithful God,
by faith
may we conquer
our deepest fears.
By faithful action
may the chains of poverty be broken.
By faithful struggle
may the web of oppression be overcome.
By faithful commitment
may the walls that divide
fall.

God of power and might,
as we go round in circles,
reluctant to make choices,
hesitant to act,
as we offer what is most precious,
give to you what matters most,
open to us the sea of your mercy
and carry us home.

Daniel Berrigan

Journey blessings

In life's journey
be to me as a star;
in the wild seas
be to me as a helm.
In the times of decision
be to me as a signpost;
in times of despair
be my loving companion.

God be with you
on the road of life's suffering.
Christ be with you
in celebration.
The Spirit be with you
to encourage and bless you
at all times and in all time.

Bless O God
the journey ahead.
Bless the travelling
and the arrival.
Bless those who welcome
and those who accept hospitality,
that Christ may come among us
in journeying and in stillness.

I set the keeping of Christ about you;
I send the guarding of God with you
to possess you, to protect you,
to accompany you
on all your paths,
through trouble, through danger, through loss.
And I set the dancing of the Spirit around you
to comfort and gladden and inspire you,
each day, each night,
each night, each day.

Birth blessing

As I cup my hand
around your head
    little one,
may God hold you
and keep you.

As I rock you
in my arms
    little one
may Christ shield you,
and encompass you.

As I bend to kiss your cheek
    little one
may the Spirit bless you
and encourage you.

Toy blessing

God bless to you
this doll little one.
May (s)he bring you joy.

God bless to you
this toy little one.
May (s)he teach you tenderness
and encourage your imagination
to soar.

Meal blessing

Bless this table
bless this door
bless the friends
who enter here;
bless the talk
   around the food
and bless this home
   for evermore.

Blessing for a work day

May God bless you
as you manage your work,
as you take painful decisions.
May God bless you
as you relate to others,
and give you strength for the day ahead.

On a child leaving home

Go carefully little one.
May your journey be safe,
your arrival secure.
May the guarding of the great God
be between your shoulders,
the justice of the gentle God
be in your footstep,
the love of the compassionate God
be in your hands.
May God protect you
in every situation
and grace you
to give and receive blessing.

God be with you in every pass,
Jesus be with you on every hill;
God be with you in every street,
Jesus be with you in every meeting;
God be with you in every difficulty,
Jesus be with you in every storm;
The Sacred Three surround and save you,
this day and through all your tomorrows.

Post-Communion

Like grapes on a sun-drenched hill
we, who came as individuals,
are now made one,
abiding in Christ
who dwells in us.
Our thirst is quenched,
the bread of life has filled us.
May we leave this table
restored and committed
to serve with justice
the thirsty and empty,
with whom we are now embodied.
In the name of Christ, bread-giver
and strengthener.

Lord Jesus Christ
you have put your life into our hands;
now we put our lives into yours.
Take us, renew us, remake us.
What we have been is past,
what we shall be, through you, still awaits us.
Lead us on.
Take us with you.

As you have been fed at this table
go feed the hungry.
As you have been set free
go to set free the imprisoned.
As you have received – give.
As you have heard – proclaim.
And the blessing which you have received
from Creator, Son and Spirit
go with you.

Encompassing presence

Ever-present Shield,
your canopy of stars covers us.
We sense your encompassing presence
in the thrill of beauty,
in the urgent claims of the poor
and deep within our hearts.
The poverty of our response,
O God of the living,
brings us to our knees.

Christ, our Friend,
we see your face
in a crowded street.
We sense your presence
in a generous action,
the costly offering,
in the sharing of a cloak
and the pouring of wine.

Spirit of Comfort,
we search for you
in the wakeful dead of night,
in the surge of bitter loneliness,
in the pain of death's betrayal
and in the smoking fires of nations at war.

Shield and Friend and Comforter,
encompass us with your presence:
go before us,
be beside us,
move within us and around us.

Be present,
Trinity of Peace,
until our journey is ended
and we see you face to face.

Special pleading

Once more –
to see a snowdrop
to smell the sea
once more
once more
to hold the child
to be a wordsmith
once more
once more
to dance a reel
dive into a pool
once more
once more
once more, O Lord
once more.

Maranatha

Come God,
        come with the frightened,
        come with the poor,
        come with the homeless,
        come with the children,
come and lead us to where you are living
and show us what you want us to do.

Lord Christ, Son of the Father, giver of the Spirit,
our world waits for your peace, for your pardon,
and for your grace. Even so come, Lord Jesus.

On retirement

God bless you
as you embrace the future.
God bless you as you lay down the past.
God bless you in the present moment
with lively hope and hopeful life.

The time that's left

God bless to me the time that's left:
to hold the child,
to see another spring,
to tidy my room,
to forgive and forget,
to reach out and befriend,
to live my life in peace and joy.
God bless to me
eternity.

Stay

Mysterious God, confounding our expectations,
meeting us where we least expect to find you,
stay with us now.

Child of the manger, healing our pain,
sharing our weakness,
stay with us now.

Source of life,
birth of God within our own experience,
stay with us now.

Stay with us in our frailty,
stay with us on our journey,

walk beside us,
live within us,
lead us to glory,
lead us.

Trust

Lord of the ages,
you are our beginning and our end.
Everlasting God,
we place our days within your care.
Eternal Father, we trust you.
For your faithfulness in the past, we thank you;
for your constant care, we praise you;
for our future in your love, we place ourselves
into your keeping
and offer our lives for your service;
through Jesus Christ, your eternal Son,
our Saviour.

May God keep us in all our days.
May Christ shield us in all our ways.
May the Spirit bring us healing and peace.
May God the Holy Trinity
drive all darkness from us
and pour upon us
blessing and light.

Endings

As you were in the ebb and flow,
as the beginning becomes the ending,
and the ending a new beginning,
be with us
ever-present God.

Wherever we go
may the joy of God the Gracious
be with us.
Wherever we go
may the face of Christ the Kindly
be with us.
Wherever we go
may the Compassion of the Spirit of Grace
be with us.
  Wherever we go
  the presence of the Trinity around us
  to bless and keep us.

We have laid our burdens down
in the presence of the living God.
We have been nourished for our journey
in the presence of the living God.
We have taken on the armour of Christ
in the presence of the living God.
Now lead us, guide us, defend us,
as we go into your world
in your name and for your sake,
O loving, living God.

Let go the past;
loosen the thongs
that bind.

Love the present;
enjoy each shining
moment.

Look to the future
with courage
and hope.

Laying down and letting go

As Columba laid down his books
and the security of a monastery,
so we lay down what is past
and look to the future.

As Aidan and Cuthbert let go
and travelled hopefully on,
so we let go hurt and pain
and travel with hope.

As Hilda changed direction
and relinquished cherished plans,
so we leave behind familiar paths
and take new steps into the unknown.

Merciful God,
for the things we have done that we regret,
    forgive us;
for the things we have failed to do that we regret,
    forgive us;
for all the times we have acted without love,
    forgive us;
for all the times we have reacted without thought,
    forgive us;
for all the times we have withdrawn support,
    forgive us;
for all the times we have failed to forgive,
    forgive us.

For hurtful words said and helpful words unsaid,
for unfinished tasks
and unrealised dreams,
God of all time
forgive us
and help us
to lay down
our burden of regret.

The above prayers may be followed by an act of contrition in which people write on a piece of paper what they wish to lay down and place it at the foot of a cross or in a boat which is launched into the sea, or in a bin to be burned. They could then place a candle by a symbol of new beginnings, like a sandal, keys, a book open at a new page.

I let go:
window and door,
house and home,
memory and fear.

I let go the hurt of the past
and look to the hope of the future.

I let go
knowing that I will always carry
part of my past with me,
woven into the story of my life.

Help me, Christ my brother,
to softly fold inside
the grief and the sadness,
to pack away the pain
and to move on;
taking each day
in your company;
travelling each step
in your love.

Facing serious illness

Out of our shock and fear
we call to you.
Out of our anger and denial
we call to you.
Out of our grief and sadness
we call to you.

(Silence)

Our eyes are heavy with tears,
our minds are racing,
our hearts thumping.

O God, where is
the joy, peace and hope
you promised?

Ever-present God,
where are you?

(Silence)

(A time to share fears and hopes, stories and worries; a time to be honest with ourselves and God. From a central candle, all light their neighbour's candle offering the light as a prayer for them.)

God comes to us
in the warmth and light
of a flickering flame,
in the cry of a child,
the smile in our neighbour's eyes.
Christ is alongside us
in our suffering.
The Spirit moves us to tears
and dries our eyes
with a breeze of comfort.

(The candles are put in a circle in the centre of
the group, perhaps during a song)

(Silence)

As surely as the tide returns to the shore,
the bird to its nest;
as surely as the sun runs its course,
so surely do I, your God and Lover,
return to you.
I will not leave you bereft.
I will weep with you.
I will dry your eyes
on the sleeve of my robe,
release what binds and poisons
your mind and your dreams.
I will come to travel with you.
You are not alone.

Come, Lord Jesus.

For mourners

Generous Creator,
out of your bounty
you bless us.

Christ the Worker,
you have brought us out of idleness
into fruitfulness.

Spirit of Comfort,
you lead us through
the tasks of mourning.

❖

God, loving N _____ ,
nearer to us than our next breath,
be with those who mourn.

Be in their shock, their grief,
their anger and despair,
that they may grieve
but not as those without hope.

Forgive all the harm we/they feel
we/they have done to N _____ and
show them that we/they are forgiven.

We offer to you
all the regrets
the memories
the pain
the 'if onlys'
knowing that you
will surround those who mourn
with your presence
and heal them and us
of all that harms us.

The future

It's hard to look to the future
when injustice rules
and nothing seems right
in ourselves or our world.

It's hard to look to the future
when each hour, each day
presents a mountain to be overcome.

In the laboured breath
of an old woman dying;
in the bitter face
of a young woman sighing;
in the cry of a child
alone in the night:

> in my breath
> my face
> my cry

hear the longing to be heard,
listen to the pain of isolation,
respond to the searching and seeking

and welcome me home.

Creator of mountains,
God of justice,
Compassionate healer,
bind up our wounds,
make straight the ways
that lead to life.

Death

*'Death is the last great festival on the road to freedom.'**

Go gently on your voyage, beloved.
Slip away with the ebb tide,
rejoice in a new sunrise.

May the moon make a path across the sea for you,
the Son provide a welcome.
May the earth receive you and the fire cleanse you
as you go from our love
into the presence of Love's completeness.

*Bonhoeffer

Into the light*

Iona
creeps up on you
round a corner in Mull.
The jetty
the Abbey
Dun I
and the village.
Such an insignificant sight
to bear the weight of history.
So small a place
to be crammed full
of visions and memories.
Beloved isle
bewitching place
of saints and sinners
strangers
and the well known ones.

Laid flat at sunset
on a calm sea.
To walk to the North End
is to walk off
the edge of the world.
To enter the womb
of the Abbey at evening
is to receive a calm
a blessing,
then to be
expelled
into the light.

* Kate's ashes were scattered on the Iona Road of the Dead during Community Week 2002.

Surrounded by a cloud of witnesses

Each occasion
we glimpse them:
that turn of a head,
that smile,
the way she walked,
his sense of humour,
each time
a knife turns
in our heart.

In time,
through the windows of our tears
we see them
and smile.
In time
we let go of sorrow.
In time
beauty and music,
remembered places,
bring solace not pain.
In your time,
God of all time,
may what we have sown in pain
be reaped in joy.

Blessings

Bless to us O God
the doors we open,
the thresholds we cross,
the roads that lie before us.
Go with us as we go,
and welcome us home.

The love of the faithful Creator,
the peace of the wounded Healer,
the joy of the challenging Spirit,
the hope of the Three in One
surround and encourage you
today, tonight, and for ever.

May God keep us in all our days,
may Christ shield us in all our ways,
may the Spirit bring us healing and peace.
May God the Holy Trinity
drive all darkness from us
and pour upon us blessing and light.

The blessing of God be yours,
the blessing of the beloved Son be yours,
the blessing of the perfect Spirit be yours;
the blessing of the Three
be poured out upon you,
serenely and generously,
today and for ever.

Trinity

God, Father, Son and Holy Spirit,
God, Mother, Saviour and Friend,
God, Creator, Redeemer and Sustainer;
Trinity, God Three in One,
perfect community,
we worship and adore you.

Today women and men
will be dazzled by your glory.
In the bright light of your presence,
in the searing, searching light of your presence,
may we lovingly, willingly respond:
Here am I – send me.

(Silence)

Today earth and humanity
will be drawn to your cross.
As the world's foundations shake
and creation's crowning glory is stretched on a tree,
may we be brought, without blemish,
into community with Christ.

(Silence)

Today all has been revealed.
All has come together:
crib and cross and empty tomb,
garden and road and upper room.
May we in our place and time
take the yoke, hear the call
and join the community of saints.

(Silence)

The circle is complete:
the three in one
and one in three.
God ever-living
God ever-loving
God ever-present
in perfect community.

Title index

The Iona Community

The Iona Community, founded in 1938 by the Revd George MacLeod, then a parish minister in Glasgow, is an ecumenical Christian community committed to seeking new ways of living the Gospel in today's world. Initially working to restore part of the medieval abbey on Iona, the Community today remains committed to 'rebuilding the common life' through working for social and political change, striving for the renewal of the church with an ecumenical emphasis, and exploring new, more inclusive approaches to worship, all based on an integrated understanding of spirituality.

The Community now has over 240 Members, about 1500 Associate Members and around 1500 Friends. The Members – women and men from many denominations and backgrounds (lay and ordained), living throughout Britain with a few overseas – are committed to a fivefold Rule of devotional discipline, sharing and accounting for use of time and money, regular meeting, and action for justice and peace.

At the Community's three residential centres – the Abbey and the MacLeod Centre on Iona, and Camas Adventure Camp on the Ross of Mull – guests are welcomed from March to October and over Christmas. Hospitality is provided for over 110 people, along with a unique opportunity, usually through week-long programmes, to extend horizons and forge relationships through sharing an experience of the common life in worship, work, discussion and relaxation. The Community's shop on Iona, just outside the Abbey grounds, carries an attractive range of books and craft goods.

The Community's administrative headquarters are in Glasgow, which also serves as a base for its work with young people, the Wild Goose Resource Group working in the field of worship, a bi-monthly magazine, *Coracle*, and a publishing house, Wild Goose Publications.

For information on the Iona Community contact:
The Iona Community, Fourth Floor, Savoy House, 140 Sauchiehall Street,
Glasgow G2 3DH, UK. Phone: 0141 332 6343
e-mail: ionacomm@gla.iona.org.uk; web: www.iona.org.uk

For enquiries about visiting Iona, please contact:
Iona Abbey, Isle of Iona, Argyll PA76 6SN, UK. Phone: 01681 700404
e-mail: ionacomm@iona.org.uk